A Product of the System
My Life In and Out of Prison

'A lucid, often heart-wrenching account. His story is one that needed to be told and has to be read' – Jimmy Boyle, *Scotsman*

'Mark Leech is an articulate honey-tongued writer. His story travels from a childhood in care, through the nightmare of sexual abuse, the discovery of his homosexuality and prison. Rooftop protests, "shitting up", taking legal action against the authorities, suicides of friends and convictions of crimes of which he claims to be innocent. What more can happen to this man?

'But Leech is a fighter: he comes out of the book with a law degree, many articles, plays and writing awards under his belt, and many sound philosophies about the justice system and its failings' – Anna Reynolds, *Observer*

'A remarkable book by a remarkable man' – Tony Benn

'Leech depicts a culture of savagery, the horror of which is all the more breathtaking for being confined and inescapable. This extremely well articulated self portrait . . . lifts the veil on "a silent world shrouded in darkness from the public" ' – *Literary Review*

'Mark Leech's impressive achievement is to have risen above the devastation he has endured and brought upon himself . . . compulsory reading' – *The Tablet*

D1585697

Mark Leech is thirty-five and since the age of nine has spent most of his life in penal institutions of one kind or another. While in prison he has studied law to degree level. He writes regularly on prison reform for the *Guardian* and various other journals, and has written several plays. These include *Blinded by Prejudice* which won the Arthur Koestler Award for prison writing in 1991 and the BBC Television Scriptwriters' Award 1991, *Without Fear or Favour* which won the John Mortimer First Prize for Playwriting for Radio, and *The Facts Speak for Themselves* which was broadcast on Radio 4. Mark Leech is currently in HMP Glenochil.

A Product of the System

My Life In and Out of Prison

MARK LEECH

VICTOR GOLLANCZ

LONDON

With love to my father:
William Gibson

First published in Great Britain 1992
by Victor Gollancz Ltd

First Gollancz Paperback edition published 1993
by Victor Gollancz
an imprint of Cassell
Villiers House, 41/47 Strand, London WC2N 5JE

Copyright © 1992 by Mark Leech

The right of Mark Leech to be identified as author
of this work has been asserted by him in accordance
with the Copyright, Designs and Patents Act 1988

A catalogue record for this book is
available from the British Library

ISBN 0 575 05571 5

Printed and bound in Great Britain by
Cox & Wyman Ltd, Reading, Berkshire

CONTENTS

Foreword by His Honour James Pickles 9

Preface 11

Acknowledgements 15

PART ONE: My Early Years 17

PART TWO: How Men Their Brothers Maim 45

PART THREE: Therapeutically Speaking 121

PART FOUR: Into the Home Straight 179

Epilogue 209

FOREWORD

by His Honour James Pickles

Mark Leech is a remarkable man and this is a remarkable book.

He wrote to me from prison several years ago, after reading my book *Straight from the Bench*. I was still a judge, and it is unusual to correspond with a serving prisoner, but I could see nothing wrong in it. Many letters passed between us. Mark is intelligent and articulate. He was writing articles for the *Guardian* and wanted to write plays. I sent him a radio play of mine that had been broadcast, and gave him advice on writing for radio. Mark taught me more than I taught him when writing my second book. I sent him queries about prisons, and he always replied quickly and lucidly.

Mark and I have only met once – in early 1991. He came on leave to interview me for the *Guardian* in connection with my retirement in July 1991. The article was never written, Mark having absconded soon after the interview. He states the sad reason in this book.

I gave Mark the idea for writing it, and I am glad. It makes an outstanding contribution to penal thinking. It will interest judges and magistrates, the Home Office, politicians, criminologists and many ordinary readers. It answers many of the questions we are all thinking.

Why do people take to crime? Many, as in Mark's case, because of early deprivation. Family circumstances conspired against him as he describes vividly. He has the talent to have done well from the start, but it was not enough. He went wrong through circumstances that were not his fault.

How should prisons be run? Not as they are at present. That is Mark's thesis, and it reinforces my own view. Courts have the painful duty to send people inside. We have to punish the wicked, and nothing does that like loss of liberty. The wavering have to be deterred by sentences they receive or hear about. The incorrigible who abuse liberty must lose it to protect others from them.

Once a sentence is passed, a court has no control over the prisoner. I went round every type of prison and was often dismayed by what was or was not happening there. For example at Ranby, a semi-open prison between Worksop and Retford – not over-crowded – when I asked what they were trying to do with the men, the answer was that they were 'keeping them until it's time to let them out'. That is not good enough.

Mark's account of prison life is vivid. Prisoners are herded about as cattle are, and brutalised as they are not. It is easy to understand how he came to hate the system and became a leading trouble-maker. Inmates should be dealt with more humanely and given responsibility in running their prisons.

Can hardened prisoners be reformed? Mark shows how it can be done – he was on the way to doing it himself. The regime at Grendon Underwood prison changed his life. There should be more places like that, where prisoners are taught to look into themselves and take a new direction. Instead of being a hopeless case, Mark became a writer with every prospect of making good in the media on his release. How his hopes were set back makes gloomy reading, but he does not flinch from the facts.

I hope that Mark will yet succeed in living a good, happy life, in freedom. He has a real contribution to make on so many issues surrounding the big social problem of our time: the explosion of crime. There are further books, articles and plays for Mark Leech to write. For the present we should be grateful for what he has already given us in this unique book.

PREFACE

Each narrow cell in which we dwell
Is a foul and dark latrine,
And the fetid breath of living death
Chokes up each grated screen,
And all but lust is turned to dust
Inside Humanity's Machine.

Oscar Wilde
The Ballad of Reading Gaol

Seventy years ago, in 1922, Sydney and Beatrice Webb wrote in their study of the English prison system, *English Prisons Under Local Government*:

> Since 1878 the prison has become a silent world, shrouded so far as the public are concerned in almost complete darkness.

This indictment of our penal system remains as true today as when it was first written. The prison is still a silent world shrouded in darkness from the public who are forced to pay for it. It is a society in the midst of public society, but closed to scrutiny and probing questions; it is also, according to one recent authority, 'where one section of the British public lives under totalitarian rule'.

Many books have been written about the deplorable conditions within our prison system, and many column inches have been daily used in cataloguing its decay and collapse. However, while the millions of words about the penal system have been penned by some eminent authors, the majority of accounts lack one essential element: personal experience of imprisonment within the penal system. A book written by a prison visitor may well be able to identify some areas of concern within the penal system, but it is a poor substitute for one written by a person who lives as well as works within it.

I make no effort to conceal that I have had experience of the prison system, indeed I believe that this will add to, rather than subtract from, the quality and character of this book. Though I claim no accolade for it, I have been a prisoner in many of our prisons. I have experienced the calm and progressive attitudes of prisons such as Maidstone and Grendon Underwood, as well as the chilling and thoroughly degrading brutality of prisons such as Dartmoor, Wandsworth and Barlinnie, to name but three. I have been in the overcrowded local prisons (those that service the main city-centre courts) such as Manchester, Durham, Birmingham, Liverpool, Bristol, Wormwood Scrubs and Brixton, in addition to the maximum security 'dispersal' prisons of Long Lartin and Parkhurst. At the opposite end of the security spectrum I have been in 'open' prisons, such as Leyhill, and in the 'closed' Scottish prisons at Inverness, Perth, Edinburgh and Glasgow.

It is this 'hands on' experience which is conspicuously lacking in books written about the prison system by academic 'experts', though this book is not the first of its kind. Jimmy Boyle in both his epics (*A Sense of Freedom* and *The Pain of Confinement*) detailed his brutal treatment at the hands of the Scottish Prison Service, while John McVicar (in *McVicar*) catalogued his horrific experiences south of the border. I could not hope to better their efforts.

For that reason a large proportion of this book is devoted to the 'therapeutic' regime of HM Prison Grendon Underwood. No other prisoner in its thirty-year history has detailed the experience of being inside Britain's only therapeutic prison; a place where the sub-culture of the main prison system is turned completely on its head in a bewildering array of psychological tests and group therapy meetings.

You will travel with me from my unhappy childhood memories in Manchester to the present day. You will learn how at the age of ten I was placed in the care of the Local Authority – though in my case you can substitute the word 'abuse' for 'care'. You will see how I have been brutalised and how I in return have brutalised others. Along the way you will discover why you so frequently see the grievances of Britain's prisoners being broadcast from bed linen draped across riot-torn prison rooftops, and you will discover what has to be done to remedy the problem rather than simply to repair the damage caused by each riot.

I reveal things in this book that I have kept secret for almost twenty years and which largely contributed to making me into the animal that I had by the age of twenty-seven undoubtedly become. Its title was selected with care for the book provides some insight into why the governor of Dartmoor Prison, on 22 February 1984, was able to describe me in an official report as 'a thoroughly offensive, dangerous and disruptive man'; and why, what's more, he was correct. Thankfully, that was not to be the final definition. Six years later another Home Office official, in yet another official report, was able to say of me: 'A mainstay of the B Wing Community, a man who has made excellent progress in therapy and who is destined to make a great success of his life. His record proves that Grendon Underwood can and does work.'

My travels between these two official extremes carry with them a lot of hard work, many restless nights and a painfully searching self-scrutiny. My life in prison has been character-ised by riots, sit-down protests and rooftop demonstrations, more than thirty successful legal battles against the Home Office fought in every arena from the County Court to the House of Lords, and more than two years spent on 'the Ghostrain': being moved, at roughly monthly intervals be-tween prisons up and down the country, often at night and always without notice, and at each new destination being held in solitary confinement for the 'Good Order and Discipline' of the prison. From all that came a man who was bitter and twisted; truly a product of the system.

This book then is my story. It is not my apology and nor is it intended to solicit your sympathy; what happened to me is still happening to hundreds of children and adults up and down the country and most, if not all, are destined to spend their lives trapped in a destructive cycle of revenge and rebellion. We must not allow that to continue.

If you put this book down having learnt a little more about the dangers that exist for our children in 'care', if you feel more enlightened about the important issues which are part and parcel of our failure to create a humane and reforming penal system – for which we all ultimately pay in many tragic ways – then the hard work that went into writing it will have been more than repaid.

ACKNOWLEDGEMENTS

To me this is the most important page in the whole book for it provides me with an opportunity to say thank you to all those people who have in many and various ways helped to make it a reality. My thanks fall into a number of categories:

To friends Stephen Sedley QC, Tim Owen, Edward Fitzgerald, Gerald Clarke, Kate Akester, Lynne Griffiths, Deirdre Haigh, Charles Knox, Ian Moir and Ronald Bain (lawyers). Dr Stephen Shaw (Prison Reform Trust), Mervyn Barrett (NACRO), Councillor Ken Murray (Strathclyde Regional Council), Joe Chapman, Ian Booth, John Keen and Ashley Lindsay (HMP Grendon Underwood), Val Maltby, Marian Liddiard, Les Douglass, Bob Farrow, Stuart Sole, Eric Allison, Geoff Coggan, Andy Bell, Phil Allen, Ned Chaillet, John Brownlow and Katrina Whone (for their respective inspiration), Tony Hewitt (Bristol Drugs Project), my literary agent Andrew Lownie and commissioning editor at Gollancz, Joanna Goldsworthy (for their patience and faith) and last, but by no means least, His Honour James Pickles, who first planted the seed which grew into this book.

To special friends B Wing Community, HMP Grendon Underwood (1989).

But my chief thanks must go to all those people who have stood by me and believed in me when I gave them more than enough reason to turn away: my father William Gibson, and my two closest friends, Arthur and Pat Wilson.

To each and every one of you – and the many more who helped, advised and inspired but who wish to remain anonymous – I extend my deepest thanks and gratitude.

PART ONE

My Early Years

I committed my first criminal offence at the tender age of six. The wooden spoon that was always used by my Irish Catholic mother to stir the rice pud was my intended victim; I hated that spoon with a ferocity I find hard to describe.

My mother, Florence, was not in a healthy state when I was born, and, tired out and near to the end of her own life, took the wooden spoon to me and made me pay with the skin of my backside for any misdemeanour. To my six-year-old eyes she looked good for another fifty years and so, I concluded, the spoon had to go.

The demise of the spoon was planned with as much military precision as a six-year-old could muster. On 'D' Day I lay in my bed and listened to the sound of the front door closing behind my father, William, who was leaving on his fourteen-mile cycle ride to the Manchester steel mills of Trafford Park; the coast was clear, it was five a.m.

I crept downstairs, trying not to trip over the huge pyjama bottoms which belonged to my elder brother. I crept into the kitchen and carefully placed the chair under the rack above the stove where the spoon sought sanctuary after its many and varied activities. With the offending instrument in my hands I moved into the living room, where the fire which my father had set before he went out was burning brightly in the grate. I aimed with care and watched the spoon fall into the middle of the flames; I did not move again until I was absolutely certain the demon was dead. I crept back upstairs and slid ecstatically between the sheets. Mission accomplished – the spoon was gone!

But mothers are both resourceful and unpredictable, a conclusion I reached many times during the eight years in which I had one. Just three days later, to my horror, the spoon was reincarnated, and she chased me all over the house with it in her hand. My mother has now been dead for a quarter of a century and, at thirty-three, I can still vividly remember that spoon and it is probably the reason why I have never eaten rice pud since. My mother now lies in her grave not 250 yards from the room in which she gave birth to me in Withington Hospital, Manchester, in the early hours of Thursday, 3 October, 1957.

My parents' marriage did not bear the stamp, 'Produce of Heaven'. An alliance between an Irish Catholic and a Protestant was an unlikely basis for a lasting loving relationship, and my father has since told me that it was the worst mistake of his life. My mother, born in March 1910, had previously been married to a Joe Laylor (of whom I have never even seen so much as a photograph) and when he died in 1939 my mother was left to cope with her two young daughters, Mary and Florence junior.

In June 1941 my mother gave birth to my sister Yvonne and two months later married Yvonne's father William Gibson, then a steel worker aged twenty-eight who came from the same Hulme district of Manchester as my mother. Soon after their marriage they moved house – the first of many moves – to 15 Peach Street in the Moss Side area of the city, and it was there that my only brother Billy was born, followed shortly after by my sister Kathy.

When I came along much later, in 1957, my mother was already well into her forties and was seeing her doctor regularly because of thrombosis and heart problems. The sisters and brother who surrounded me were up to sixteen years older than me, a gap which became more apparent as the first five years of my life slipped by. My father is a kind, caring and hardworking man, but he was little match for my mother, who was always firmly in control.

My mother, who regularly predicted that I would be the death of her, was not a pleasant woman, but I realise now – with the soft gloss of understanding with which we all try to cover up unpleasant memories of the past – that I came along too late in her life. She was well past ideal child-bearing age and her illnesses only added to her already formidable difficulties. At that time in her life the last thing she needed was to be bestowed with the pressures and responsibilities of a new child.

My mother was staunchly catholic in her views and her five-foot-two-inch frame concealed a powerhouse of energy; there was never the slightest doubt that she was the one who made the decisions affecting our future. We moved house a number of times during my early years and our changes of residence were, according to my father at least, the result of my mother's 'gypsy blood'. One day my father arrived home from work 'to be told as soon as I'd got through the front door that she'd found another house just 200 yards up the road'. She had already fixed the date for the move and ordered the removal van; my father was given 'advance notice' only so he could book the day off work to help. That was the only time they 'discussed' the move, which went ahead a week later; my mother's decision-making process did not involve consultation, nor did it invite or welcome comment.

During the school summer holidays before my seventh birthday, my mother became more and more short-tempered as the house became crowded with people, and the endless arguments between her and my father which then began went on long into the nights. My brother Billy, who had just joined the Royal Navy, was home on leave, Kathy had Beatles pop music blaring out most of the day, and my eldest sister Yvonne had returned home after a short-lived marriage to a man called Bill Green, proudly assuring my mother that she was 'still Virgo Intacta'. While that appeared to please my mother, it baffled me, and my enquiries at school, 'Miss, are you still Virgo Intacta?', did not endear me to my teacher.

I was passed from brother to sister and my mother's motto – 'Will you just look after Mark' – became the signal for the house to be evacuated. They all developed an aversion to me which, I suspect, remains with them to this day. To be fair, I can understand their reaction, for they were all at an age when they were much more interested in youth clubs and the opposite sex than, to quote Kathy, 'being lumbered with *him* again'.

As a result of this impasse, my mother took to turning me out of the front door, easing her conscience by calling it 'playing out'. From an early age, therefore, I made my friends on the street and not in the home; the local shopping centre, Sale Circle, became my playground, while 'home' meant little more than my bedroom.

One day the local newsagent, Mr Carew, a great strapping man with an equally oversized moustache, bought a free-standing bubble-gum machine which he placed proudly outside his shop. It was but one week old when in an effort to 'fix' it, because it had swallowed my penny without subsequent reward, I pushed it over. I knew what I had done the moment I saw it begin to topple over and I stood there transfixed as this one-legged monster obeyed the laws of gravity and then vomited its contents all over Sale Circle. I ran home for dear life.

My red hair has always been my downfall for it is impossible to be inconspicuous when you have what amounts to a Belisha beacon on your head. I reached the safety of my bedroom in record time and sat peeping out of the curtains to see if I'd been followed. I knew trouble lay ahead when I saw Mr Carew striding purposefully towards my home.

It may have been too much in one day for my mother, I don't know, but the result was my first ever meeting with the wooden spoon. I was left shocked and sore. My mother – unlike my brother and sisters – had never given me anything but a clip behind the ear before so this marked a new milestone along the road of my life and unfortunately it became more the rule than the exception during the next two years.

The thrashing with the spoon was over long before my father arrived home and he was instructed to take me to the newsagent's to apologise for what I had done. He went up a mile in my estimation when he told the newsagent that the machine should have been set in concrete. Mr Carew was not impressed and replied, pointing at me, 'If anything should be set in concrete it should be that little bugger' – an idea which many in authority have since found sympathy with. It was then that I set about planning my first criminal offence – 'the mysterious disappearance of the spoon' as my mother was to call it a few months later, while staring intently into my ever-innocent eyes.

As the summer wore on and everyone got on everyone else's nerves, the parental arguments continued long into the nights. I never knew what they were about – and despite the volume at which they were conducted I doubt whether anyone else had much of an idea either. I used to sit at the top of the stairs in my brother's pyjamas, listening while the two people upon whom I relied most in this increasingly baffling and complex world tore each other to pieces.

I gradually learnt the lesson that grown-ups in general, and the parental variety in particular, were not to be trusted. They were contradictory beings who preached one thing and practised another. 'Always be honest' I was instructed by my mother, who spent her housekeeping money down at the Bingo and never told my father about it until the day they came to turn off the electricity. 'Don't smoke' was another gem she passed on to me, while puffing her way through forty a day. 'Always keep your promises' – but her actions did not match her words. It was all too much for my young brain to comprehend, and I withdrew confused and having learnt the lesson that 'authority' was not a nice thing to come into contact with. So I spent more and more time 'playing out' and less and less time at home; and it suited me just fine.

The school I attended, St Aidens RC Primary (mother got her way as always), became my best friend. I would sit for hours in the playground long after everyone else had packed up and gone home, soaking up the peace and quiet of the late afternoon and early evening and delaying for as long as possible the moment when I would have to go home.

Three days after my eighth birthday, in October 1965, we made our 200-yard house move to 8 Barry Road from our old house at 8 Pingot Avenue, in the Northern Moor district of Manchester. My mother had recently returned from a trip to the USA where she had been visiting my stepsister Mary who had emigrated there four years before, and I noticed that she was now going to the hospital more frequently, for what she termed 'me chick-ups'.

On Friday, 4 February 1966, my father slept in my bedroom, taking his first day's holiday in years that was not the result of moving home, because my mother was not feeling well. I slept soundly enough but was woken up a little after seven by a sound which even now I can only describe as a 'bump'. I got out of bed and together with my dad went next door to my mother's room to investigate. She was lying on the floor on the far side of the bed, quite dead. The feelings inside me at that moment have baffled me since. I did not cry about her death, not then nor at the funeral, and in a way I was strangely relieved; she had been responsible for too much in my life that I would collectively call 'bad'.

I have often suspected that had I come along earlier in her life, ours would have been a special relationship, but in the short time we had to get to know each other, we seemed to have only bad times. Many times since have I wished she was still alive. There are so many questions that I would like to ask her. 'What was life like for you? Why did you treat me in such a way? What pressures were you under, and why couldn't you do something about them?' But the reality is that we have to leave our unanswered questions only guessed at, making the best of a mixture of experience and intuition.

The family that existed after the death of my mother was vastly different from the one that existed before it. My father, a weak-willed person though profoundly caring of his children, found his solace in drink. My brother returned to the Navy and my sisters set about creating lives of their own. I was often alone in the house late at night when my father came in drunk, covered in vomit and singing songs he'd never have got away with had my mother been around. Some nights he'd come in covered in leaves from broken bushes, the result of falling into someone's garden in his drunken attempt to find his way home. It's now a standing joke with my father that he is the only person in Manchester ever to have suffered from 'privet rash'! But, whatever the humour in the scenario, life for me had taken a turn for the worse.

One thing that can be said about my mother is that she always kept us clean and we never went short of food. With mother gone the family collapsed in on itself and found only a massive void. My father tried to cook and we ended up with white chips. My mother's sister, Eileen – who had spent most of her life as a governess in the Philippines – briefly came to stay but found it too hard to adjust to life on the shop floor and left within a few weeks.

Children can be callous, because they do not appreciate how they can cause hurt, and I often ended up rolling around the playground with those who thought it funny to make jokes about the clothes I was wearing or the free school-meals I had to have since my father was no longer working. The love I once had for my school began to evaporate and at this point I began to stay away. I used to stay out all day and long into the nights. The lock on our front door had been broken for months – and stayed that way for years – and a hefty shove was all that was required to gain entry when I chose to go home.

My truanting from school brought me to the attention of the various social agencies then in existence to monitor it and, within a few weeks, I was called from my bed one morning by my father who told me that the young man seated opposite had come to take me 'away'. The man was Peter Morgan, of the Yewtree Lane Child Guidance Clinic just around the corner. Not trusting adults, I viewed their promises that things would be 'better' with more than a little scepticism. All the nine-year-old could hear was, once again, the plain message, 'you're not wanted here'. Looking back I can see that there were genuine reasons why I could not remain at home, but I did not have powers of perception in excess of my years and I had then to make of it what I could. I also realise now that what took place later was not what any of them would have wished, and they would have stopped it had they known, but the cumulative effect of my years in 'care' was that my belief was reinforced that you do not trust anyone with authority – they always abuse it.

My first port of call in the 'care' of the Local Authority was an assessment centre called Broome House, on Wilmslow Road in the leafy Manchester suburb of West Didsbury. I don't recall a great deal about Broome House because I wasn't there for long, but it was a huge mansion which housed a goose called Miranda – who kept everyone awake at night – and a donkey called Felix who had a fetish for curry! From Broome House I was sent to a boarding school in Cheshire which I will, for reasons which will become obvious later, call by an invented name: Lakeview House.

Lakeview was a new experience; it showed me what life could be like – in more ways than one. It was a stately home set in its own parkland and offered outward-bound activities. Suddenly there were horses to ride, hikes to go on, canoeing, abseiling, rock-climbing – everything the snotty-nosed kid from the backstreets of Manchester had never had before. I threw myself into it with all the energy and vigour I could muster, loving every minute. Each day was split into two, with classwork in the morning and activities in the afternoon.

By my eleventh birthday I had swum a mile non-stop, walked the 250 miles of the Pennine Way in eighteen days, learnt how to play rugby, skin a rabbit, set a trap, pitch a tent, survive in the open, map-read, and 101 other things which I am surprised ever came my way. The school horses, of which there were seven, were ridden as frequently as possible and were also employed to pull the traps when the hay-making season arrived and we all had to work long into the evenings. During my first term I started to play rugby and took to it immediately; later it always seemed silly to kick a ball when you could pick it up and run with it.

The school year was divided into three terms and at the end of my first term I was told that I would spend the holidays with my eldest sister Yvonne, who had recently married for the second time – a chap called Kevin – and was now managing a Victoria Wine shop opposite Pendleton Church in Salford. The decision had been made by my sister and the Manchester Social Services, but no one thought to consult me. I counted the days to the end of term like all the other boys in the school, but for me it was not with a longing to be home among a loving family, but with a dread of leaving for three whole weeks the school that had so soon become so precious to me.

Once in my room on the first night at my sister's, I carefully slipped down the back stairs and disappeared out of the door. By 5 a.m. the following morning I had walked and hitched the thirty-five miles back to Lakeview and was discovered asleep in my bed a few hours later by a cleaner who was absolutely astounded to find me there. Once they had discovered me there was little that anyone could do but take me back to Yvonne's – but I was back at school again the very next day and at that point my housemaster stepped in. Mr Robinson, a towering Irishman who knew absolutely everything, lived with his wife in a flat at the top of the school. The Robinsons said I could stay with them for the remainder of the school holiday, and I jumped at the chance. The Robinsons were tremendous people, who understood what I had been going through and who repaid the trust I put in them many times over. I was happy, but fate was preparing to deal me another of those blows that it has a habit of doing every now and again: the tables were once more set to turn.

It was a beautifully sunny day, two months into the new term, and I had just been out to feed the horses. Everyone at school was excited at the prospect of a camping trip the following week. The Robinsons had taken two weeks' holiday and were due to return the following afternoon. The news broke at about 3 p.m. They had both been killed in a car accident on the outskirts of St Malo in Brittany. The whole school was numb with shock. But Lakeview was no ordinary school. It taught its pupils to be self-reliant and to cope with hardships, and we carried on as best we could, while I replayed my recent memories of the Robinsons, memories I treasure to this day.

At the end of next term it became clear that I would have to go and stay with Yvonne and Kevin, who had given up the wine shop after the recent birth of their daughter Lisa, and were now living in a two-bedroomed terraced house – fondly referred to by Yvonne as 'Crap Creek' – close to the once-famous Manchester fun-fair of Belle Vue. It was probably the most difficult three weeks of my life so far, but I'd promised I would stay there and I did, although I was itching to get back and was at the coach station a good three hours before the bus was due to leave for Lakeview.

The start of the new term coincided with my tenth birthday and the arrival of the Robinsons' replacement, Mr Lewis (not his real name). He was in his mid-twenties, single, keen on all sports and outdoor pursuits and with an accent that at first I found difficult to understand. I was later told it was Geordie, but was none the wiser. Mr Lewis took over the Robinsons' flat at the top of the school building and I helped him to move his boxes into the rooms which held so many pleasant memories for me.

I was captain of the under-11 rugby team at that time and as it was Mr Lewis's favourite sport he very quickly took a shine to me. Close to Lakeview was another school which we frequently played at sports. On one Sunday morning when we played them at rugby I injured my back in a scrum and had to go off. We still won, and by a remarkable margin, so don't get the impression that I was the best in the team! Later Mr Lewis asked me to go up to his flat so that he could examine my back. I lay on the bed, stripped to the waist, and he began to rub liniment into my back and massage the area that had been hurt that morning in the scrum. That was as far as it went on that occasion, but the time soon came when, in the evenings, he would invite me to his flat to watch a programme called 'The High Chaparral'; it was on BBC2 and the school television did not have the aerial necessary to receive it.

Mr Lewis liked me a great deal and I enjoyed this feeling of being wanted. It was a feeling I had not experienced much before. Before too long things developed to the stage where we would play 'games' after the TV programme was over; and Blind Man's Buff went a little further than it should have done when he began to fondle me each time I was 'caught'. That was the innocent beginning of the sexual abuse which continued for the next three years and took place four times a week. I knew what we were doing was wrong, I knew it was not supposed to happen, but at that time I needed to be important in *someone*'s life.

The abuse began with his convincing me that what we were doing was special, and just between the two of us. He knew that the last thing I wanted was to be sent home, and he told me that that would be the consequence if 'our secret' ever became known. I made sure that never happened.

Later in life I covered this period in depth, and though I

have tried hard to analyse my feelings they are difficult to define. I enjoyed the feeling of being wanted, and that made the abuse somehow special to the ten-year-old boy who needed that security in his life. But the grim reality was that I lay on my stomach four nights of the week for three years, while he used my body as little more than a receptacle. To me the half-hour of abuse was worth the twenty-three-and-a-half hours of feeling wanted. The first time I saw blood in my underpants I was terrified. I went to see Mr Lewis and I remember his words as if they were spoken yesterday: 'Oh, it's nothing, all perfectly normal.' In the words of Mandy Rice-Davies, 'Well, he would say that, wouldn't he?'

My concern at the time was to avoid being sent home and I took great care to ensure that the meetings with Mr Lewis never came out in conversation and so remained 'our secret'. I put up with the raging emotions which the abuse ignited within me. If this is what had to be done, then I would do it; the alternative was to go 'home' to a world which I did not want to be a part of, where I was not wanted and was not consulted, where, in Yvonne's philosophy, 'little kids should be seen and not heard'.

The churning emotions are difficult to explain to anyone who has not been sexually abused. The feeling of having your body taken over by someone else for their own purposes and pleasure has to be experienced to be understood. It cannot be fully realised—at least not to any satisfactory degree—by anyone who has not experienced for themselves the brutal horror which is sexual abuse or rape. As I lay on my stomach, with the grunts and the groans, the whispers in my ear and the sweat on my body, I tried hard to reconcile how this man, who told me many times that he 'loved' me, could demonstrate that love in a way which caused me so much pain. This was another situation I could not understand. I tried hard but it was beyond me. I knew from the Robinsons that love could exist, but I simply could not equate that with the searing pain I felt each time he plunged into my body; that is sexual abuse, and for 'love' read 'lust'.

As the months rolled by and the abuse continued, I became

more and more mixed up in myself. My sporting activities suffered and I lost the captaincy of the rugby team. Though I never discussed it with anyone, I suspected that Mr Lewis was sharing 'our secret' with other boys in the school. Gradually, as the terms turned into years and I became older, I began to find myself being pushed away. No longer did I feel special or wanted, and those long-since-forgotten feelings of rejection made an unwelcome return to my life. I began to smoke when I was thirteen and I found the shower room – where I always went after visiting Mr Lewis – an ideal place to be alone and to conceal the smoke from my illicit cigarettes.

One evening after I had not been to his flat for a week, I plucked up the courage to visit him without invitation; something I had always been told not to do. He was extremely angry when he opened the door and told me in no uncertain terms to go away, which I did, but not before I caught a glimpse of the boy sitting on his bed. I was devastated.

Suddenly everything I had believed in, all that I had come to love and cherish in my young life, fell down around my ears. The lesson I had learnt as a child at home was painfully relearnt: you must not trust those in authority. I had been misled into thinking that I was cared for and that my efforts to please were appreciated. It was a crushing realisation for the thirteen-year-old that this was not the case, and it took me the best part of the next twenty years to get over it.

Sitting there that evening, alone in the shower room, the tears fell freely. I suddenly hated the school I had come to love. I knew that I no longer had feelings for it and I wanted to destroy it all. I ripped out all the fixtures and fittings in the shower changing room and then set fire to the towel rack before leaving; almost a replica of the ritual burning of the spoon seven years before. I ran away from Lakeview many times after that, my school work deteriorated, I was abusive to all I came into contact with and I trusted no one but myself. No one stopped to ask why; it was just put down to a 'phase' I was going through.

On one of my 'escapes' I stole a bicycle from outside the school. This, coupled with my behaviour at Lakeview, qualified me for a place in an approved school; society washed its hands of me and surrendered me to a criminal justice system which was destined not so much to reform my behaviour, as to make it considerably worse. The lesson has to be learned that casting young offenders into institutions does not cure the escalating crime rate – it causes it.

West Bank approved school sits just outside the suburb of Stockport on the outskirts of what is now Greater Manchester. The school was Roman Catholic orientated, with most of the teaching being carried out by a resident group of nuns. The school's housemaster, Leo Corcoran, was a man difficult to dislike. He was a very hard man, who believed in strict discipline, but he did not use volume to mask a lack of intelligence like so many of his peers. He treated his group of thirteen-year-olds like men – a practice which earned him the nickname Sergeant.

This environment was vastly different to anything I had experienced before. No longer could you go for walks when you wanted. You had instead to earn points on a merit system and only those in the top 'merit grade' could have the privilege of freedom on a Saturday. It took me many months to reach the position where I was eligible to go home, but the visits were always an anticlimax. Dad would either be in bed or down the pub and Kathy had a full-time job at British Debt Services in the city centre. Generally the house was as cold and empty as it had always been for me, and my friends had either moved or no longer considered me a part of their group.

At school I began to learn many things about crime. I could professionally hotwire a car at thirteen and drive one expertly a year later. The school was also different in that there was clearly a them-and-us divide between the keepers and the kept; a divide which grew stronger the longer you were there. On the weekends when I couldn't go home because of my behaviour, I would hang around the school and get into mischief; a practice which only ensured that the following weekend was spent in the same way.

I was at West Bank less than a year before it closed down and I had my first experience of being 'ghosted' – something which was later to become run of the mill for me. One evening we were all called together and told that the school was closing down the next day. I was dispatched the following morning to St Georges approved school in Freshfield on the outskirts of Liverpool and found myself mixing with those people collectively known as Scousers; the most comical group of people I have ever met. Their innate sense of humour, coupled with a professional cunning, made St Georges into one huge Fagin's kitchen. I had moved up a league by going to St Georges as they catered for boys up to sixteen – which seemed ancient to me at the time.

Homosexuality is no longer a taboo subject, except to those who suffer enormous guilt over things they have done themselves. I know from my own experience that homosexuality is rife in any all-male environment. Of course there were some, though not many, who did not take part, but they were – particularly at that age – very much in the minority. Strangely, those who did 'dabble' but found it hard to come to terms with later were usually those who went around shouting about 'poofs' and 'queers'; a comical chant of guilt, nothing more.

St Georges was no different in this respect. Homosexuality was practised and, as the school contained boys who were well into puberty, sex was a subject which was completely in fashion. Whether we spoke of girls we pretended, with great conviction, that we had 'done it' with, or whether it was simply an expressed emotional wish for the future, it was discussed. Homosexual 'dabbling' took place and I joined in on a number of occasions. The rooms were small and while it was not done openly there were places to go which were common knowledge – even if many would deny it later. I have over the years since seen many of the lads from St Georges and we have laughed about those times; most are now married with families of their own.

When I left St Georges in April 1971 I went once more to live with Yvonne and Kevin. They had recently moved from 'Crap Creek' and were living in Roundwood Road in Northenden, a village on the southern outskirts of Manchester. I started at the local secondary modern school, St Columba's, and for a while things did get better, but the novelty soon wore off for me. I was staying out late at night, was unruly and up to my ears in crime. Yvonne predicted that I hadn't learnt my lesson and would soon be back inside; in fact I had learnt my lesson, it was simply that I had been taught the wrong lesson. Within a few weeks Yvonne and Kevin could no longer cope with my behaviour and I was sent to the Manchester Remand Home for Boys, known as Rose Hill, just 250 yards from their front door.

Many of the boys at Rose Hill, a mansion house which once belonged to a man who owned half the railways in northern England, had been sent there by order of the courts; as a result crime was the dominant skill-area. My housemaster at Rose Hill, Roger Whiteside, was an ex-Royal Navy Petty Officer who took his task seriously. One day shortly after my arrival, just before a case conference – where they gather around a table to plan out your life in your absence – I was asked by Roger what I would like to do; this was the first time anyone had sought my views and it still stands out in my mind. My brother was still in the Navy and I expressed a wish – to which I hadn't given enough thought – to join him. It was therefore decided that I should be sent to the Naval Training Establishment on the outskirts of Bristol and I arrived there one afternoon early in February 1972.

The National Nautical School – or simply the Nash as it was known to its occupants – was designed and run as a naval ship. I obviously had grave misconceptions about it from the start for I remember arriving in a car and wondering where the 'ship' was, without realising I was already on board it!

My time at the Nash was destined to be short. The place

was wall-to-wall discipline, which is hardly my favourite subject. I had learnt to question absolutely everything that those in authority told me; they *always* had some ulterior motive, it was simply a question of finding it. Unfortunately naval discipline was not designed to cope with the searching inquiries of a stroppy fourteen-year-old and I was given enough extra duties to last me until I was an Admiral.

In addition to the usual naval niceties of bulling boots, pressing uniforms and 'turning to' at all hours of the night for guard duty, I also had to learn the thirty-two points of the compass by heart – for which my pay increased by a huge six pence per week. There were also parade-ground drills, assault courses, scrubbing out the barracks – and boat pulling, a euphemism for bloody hard graft, which consisted of going down to the local docks each afternoon where our huge five-ton lifeboat was sitting on the ebbing tide.

The dock was a good 400 yards long and sixteen of us, stripped to the waist, would pull that boat for all we were worth. Up and down the dock we would go, steaming with exertion, guided always by the irrepressible 'Commie John'; not a Russian, but Commander Johnson, our teacher. He was every inch the seaman, with a Captain Birdseye beard, snow white except for the portions under his nose which were brown from the Woodbines he used to smoke and whose ends we pocketed for a secret drag in the evenings.

My naval career came to an abrupt end after I had decided that I had had quite enough of this authoritarian regime; if this was the Royal Navy – which it wasn't – then give me civilian life. I left the Nash after I had gone AWOL and 'borrowed' a car to take me from Bristol to Manchester; using a skill I had acquired in the approved schools. The captain of the Nash was not at all sympathetic: 'If you want sympathy, you'll find it in the dictionary between shit and syphilis', as he put it. I hated their authoritarian regime; they disliked this questioning teenager who would trust no one – the parting was as certain as it was mutually necessary.

Theft of the motor car qualified me for entry to a borstal, and so I left behind one uniform only to climb into another. I was first sent to the Borstal Allocation Centre (BAC) at Strangeways Prison in Manchester, my first taste of imprisonment and I could not have chosen a more brutal establishment for my debut. The BAC at Strangeways occupied, in those days, the wings of the prison known as G, H and K. It has long since disappeared with the demise of the Borstal Service but it taught me much about the 'system' which, for the next fifteen years, was to become such a fundamental part of my life – and changing it was to become my vocation.

I was locked in a cell that first night with two others who were also destined for borstal. I had never set eyes on either of them before and we had nothing more to keep us company than a piss-pot which, from the stench it gave off, had not been cleaned out in a year. The prison officers paraded around the landing as if it was a military academy; with their big boots, long faces and slashed cap-peaks, they presented an image of intimidation. The majority looked and acted like mini-Hitlers and they were far more savage than any of those I'd met in care. We were treated in a way which bordered on sadistic and which created within me deep feelings of bitterness and resentment that a decade spent in borstal could never have obliterated. I had been in Strangeways – an appropriate name – for only a few hours when I witnessed something which I have seen many times since and have often experienced myself: brutality.

The chamber pot in the cell was full and it was approaching 6 p.m. David Cooper, a small and inoffensive lad from the Moss Side area of the city with a fetish for cashing other people's cheques, pressed the cell bell in order to ask if we could empty the pot before they locked up the prison for the evening. After two hours of ringing the bell four officers finally came to the door and hauled David out of the cell. As soon as the door closed we could hear a screw shouting 'Where's the fucking fire?', followed by shouts and screams. When David returned a few minutes later his lip was split and the blood was dripping on to his shirt. The door was closed and I got the message: the piss-pot would have to wait until morning.

As if the beating the night before was not enough, they compounded their bullying the following morning by placing David on report for 'assaulting an officer'; I don't know whether he did, but I know who had the injuries when the door opened, and who didn't. I never saw David Cooper again after that. He disappeared in the depths of the prison disciplinary system, which I shall give you a tour of later, and I was sent to Hindley Borstal on the outskirts of Wigan the following week.

Hindley Borstal in Gibson Street, opened in 1962, was surrounded by a huge wall. It housed some 400 inmates – or 'trainees' as we were more properly known. The four 'houses', North, East, South and West, were split into two groups, with North and West at one end of the huge central corridor known as the M1, and South and East at the other; I was sent to East House along with a dozen others who had come to pay their debt to society. As a borstal trainee I was to spend much of 1974 being trained in all aspects of motor-car theft, credit and cheque-book fraud, the growing of cannabis plants and a number of intricate ways of defrauding my bank if ever I could persuade a manager to allow me an account: not for nothing was Hindley known as the Northern Academy of Crime!

My first taste of being a borstal boy – for I was to have two such sentences, as you will hear – was being taken to East House and there confronted with the house senior officer. I had never seen such a man before, nor have I since. Absolutely huge, totally bald, and an expert in karate, this was Dave 'Oddjob' Hodgeson, who has since successfully represented England in many martial-arts competitions. I was puzzled when I first saw him by his wig, which was so ill-fitting that it moved about his head when he nodded or shouted. Twice I saw it fall off completely in situations in which my laughter was inappropriate to say the least. I came to know him well during the year I was at Hindley, and underneath all the bullshit and shouting – which is part of any prison officer's professional make-up – I found a kind and caring man who really wanted to help but was prevented from doing so by the constraints of the system within which he operated; constraints that remain a prominent feature of the penal system today. That first night, however, he had to make his impression and he lined all the new trainees up against the wall.

'Address every member of staff as Sir, double when you're told to double, your cell is to be left clean and tidy – no shit in the piss-pots – and if you're looking for a pleasant time here, forget it.' Months later, when I was a relatively old hand, I realised it was bullshit because he used the same address to every new recruit who came through the door. We got off to a bad start when he introduced the subject of sport: 'You play ball with me and I'll play ball with you, but never forget it's my ball you're playing with.' I've never been one for ultimatums!

Our first run-in came within a week of my arrival when I was told to report to the concrete shop for work. The workshop employed around forty prisoners and, as its name implies, its job was to turn tons of cement into paving slabs for the local council. I was not having any of that, particularly not for 75p per week. I told Oddjob that I was a vegetarian and therefore could not work in the concrete shop; steel safety boots had to be worn and because these were made out of leather, they were against my principles – I thought I was so fucking clever!

Oddjob was not at all impressed and I was taken to the punishment block that morning to face the governor, or so I thought. Oddjob believed in reasoning with people and he had his own unique way of doing it. In the block I was placed in a strip cell and the door was closed behind me. Years later the alarm bells would ring if they closed the door of a strip cell without taking the clothes off me – hence its name – but I was a naive teenager lost in the depths of my own ignorance. With the door closed I was left alone. Before too long I started to get hot. I took off my overall jacket, then the jumper and shirt and finally the overalls; I was standing dripping in sweat two hours later when they opened the door.

'Hot in here ain't it, son? Want a shower?' – something else which years later would have set the alarm bells off, since officers do not offer you anything without there being an ulterior motive somewhere. I accepted the offer of a shower and stood under the cool water, emerging totally refreshed to find I had no clothes at all. I was given a towel and taken to a second cell where I was told I would shortly receive my clothes; as soon as the door slammed shut I realised this cell had no windows and no heating.

Within ten minutes I was freezing the balls off myself, jumping around and hugging myself trying to keep both warm and a sense of decency. Even my goose pimples had goose pimples. The door opened an hour later and there stood Oddjob with a smile on his face. I asked for my clothes. 'Clothes?' he questioned. 'Can't give you any socks, they're made of wool, see, and a jumper's out of the question too for the same reason, I'm afraid. Overalls you can't have because of the leather straps and, as for boots or shoes, well you know how it is . . .' Of course I realised he was talking just as much bullshit as I had been, but he had made his point and I can take a hint. I became Ordinary Diet within the hour and dutifully reported to the concrete shop that afternoon; Hindley was not going to be the pushover I thought it would be!

I have always been a great one for reading the rules and during one of my sessions I discovered that as a member of the Mormon religion I could have cocoa with my meals instead of the dish water that passed for tea. I made my application for a change of religion – my mother must have been turning in her grave – and was seen by the chaplain, Ian Craig, the following afternoon. 'Why do you want to be a Mormon?' he asked after I had given him my name and number. I replied, quite honestly, that I preferred cocoa to tea and this was one way of getting it without having to pay for it. Later the next day, when

I heard that my application had been refused, I learnt the meaning of the ubiquitous prison phrase, 'In the discretion of the Governor'.

I left Hindley in November 1974 and travelled down to Portsmouth where I was to stay with my brother Bill and his wife Ann. My father had also moved down from Manchester to stay at my brother's and was now back on the rails with a job in the local naval base, thanks to my brother's influence. Within a few days of moving to Portsmouth I had my first sexual encounter with a girl; contrary to what you might think, I do not remember her name and the earth remained decidedly stationary. My brother was away at sea quite a lot during this period and I found a job as a parts assistant in a local garage for the princely sum of £13 per week.

My father had picked himself up from the death of my mother and subsequent redundancy and returned to his usual hard-working self. He would go down the pub a couple of nights a week for the last hour and this would leave me and my sister-in-law alone at home; Ann and Bill had two children who were both of an age when the Six O'Clock News was their late-night movie. To say I was surprised when Ann made her first pass at me would be an understatement – I was dumbstruck.

I felt embarrassed and tried to conceal it, but that made matters worse. I pretended that I had misunderstood, but she was a forceful character and much as I tried to make it clear that I wasn't interested, she pursued me. I am sure that many men would have been delighted to have taken her to bed, but not only was she my brother's wife, there was also the complication of my confused ideas about sex and my own sexual preferences; I could not deal with this. On occasions it reached almost comical proportions. I would do anything to get out of the house rather than be alone with her and I must have gone for a walk a hundred times in the short period I was living there. I was relieved when my brother returned home and was able, I guess, to answer her demands for nookie.

The presence of my brother did not make matters easier for me as we have never been close, more distant acquaintances than brothers. I felt at the age of seventeen that the time had come to branch out and find my own way in life. I took a bedsit in Nightingale Road, Southsea, and in the first few weeks of 1975 I closed the door on the world.

I had a probation officer I was supposed to see each week, but I soon found he had hundreds of others on his books and a phone call was generally sufficient to discharge my reporting obligations. Looking back I can see where the probation service should have been able to help me, but failed to do so because of a mixture of overwork and underfunding; in the years since then the situation has got worse instead of better.

I lost my job at the local garage within a few weeks because I could not keep my hands off the cars on the forecourt, taking them for joyrides when the garage was closed in the evenings. I found my next job as a carpet salesman in Elm Grove, Southsea, and increased my wages to £16 per week. The flat cost me half that and on the rest I had to live and fend for myself, which I had never done before. I had no idea about budgeting for food; it is always provided in prisons so I had little knowledge of prices and little experience of buying things. I was at a complete loss when it came to tax and insurance. With such a lack of experience of living in the 'free world' I fell back on my criminal activities quite quickly and took to 'borrowing' money from my gas meter; a fact which did not please my landlord – who dumped me and my clothes somewhat unceremoniously on the street a few weeks later.

I found my next accommodation in a guest house on the seafront in Southsea, run by two gay men, Clive and David. They took me in for minimal rent – at least in the financial sense – and though they wanted to sleep with me, they did not take advantage to excess. All that I was concerned with at that time was getting through each day as it came; life had become synonymous with survival.

I did not tell my probation officer what was going on, and neither did he seem greatly interested during our brief conversations in hearing of anything that would add to his already mammoth workload. He was content, even if I wasn't, to hear that I had survived another week without being caught with my hands in the till; in probationspeak, 'being caught' means all kinds of nasty consequences for probation officers, who then have to write reports, cover their arses and appear in court when you are sentenced.

On 1 May 1975 I found myself once again in the dock of the local magistrates' court after being caught driving a car whose removal the owner objected strongly to. I had lost my job with the carpet shop and being out of work did not increase my prospects of staying out of prison. However, I was represented by a good solicitor, Roger Salvetti from Lyndhurst Groves, who managed to persuade the beaks to give me another chance. Despite being out of work I was fined £118 – this in 1975 – and I knew as I left the court that I had not the slightest prospect of being able to pay it. It has always puzzled me why magistrates insist on imposing fines when defendants have little or no hope of paying them; it simply delays the inevitable imprisonment.

Within a few months of being fined at the court for theft of the car, the court fines officer was chasing his tail trying to locate me. At this point I decided to put into practice one of the skills which the Borstal Service had taught me, and I turned to cheque-book fraud. The judge was of the impression that I had not been paying attention to the fraud lectures and rewarded my endeavours by sending me back to borstal for more tuition.

I went to the Borstal Allocation Centre at the back of Winchester Prison; known locally as the Dolls' House because it held young offenders. In the BAC at Winchester they locked two prisoners in each small cell, no more than six foot six inches square, and they kept you there for twenty-three hours a day; there were half-a-dozen suicide attempts while I was there, two of them successful.

When you enter a penal institution, you are immediately thrust into a sharply polarised environment. Before the new arrival has been in the door twenty-four hours, he has been stripped of his name and had it replaced by a number, and his clothes are removed and replaced by cast-off clothing which frequently has no buttons and doesn't fit. He is told to obey the rules without ever being told what those rules are, and he is given a cursory medical examination by prison medical officers who have been described by their NHS colleagues as 'second-rate doctors, performing a second-rate service'. Walking in a line with other unfortunates who have suffered the same fate, he is then put into a narrow concrete box – which, contrary to general opinion, frequently doesn't even contain a pot to piss in.

He shares this box, for twenty-three hours a day, with a person he has probably never met before but has to learn to live with. He is taught to have respect for authority by suffering brutality and arrogance all wrapped up in appalling conditions. At 7.30 a.m. he will be unlocked and told to slop out the plastic pot which may have held his and his cell mate's bodily waste for anything up to sixteen hours. He will carry his pot to the recess which is often flooded because of overuse and, treading amid faeces and urine, he will add to the overflow by pouring its contents down the common sluice. When this is completed, a charming start to the day, everyone goes for breakfast.

Despite what the Home Office says about having abandoned censorship of mail, all letters to and from a prisoner – with the sole exception of letters covered by legal privilege – are routinely censored; the Home Office, when it redrafted the rules following the Woolf Report in 1990, purposely left themselves with a residual power of censorship. For the privilege of discovering the myriad rules relating to correspondence and visits to which the prisoner is subject, the Home Office charges £1. Is it really any wonder that our penal system as I write this, a year after the Woolf Report was published, is still suffering from serious riots and disturbances?

Within a few weeks of being put in the Dolls' House in Winchester, I was transported by coach with other trainees to Portland Borstal on the island of the same name just off the coast of Weymouth. Built out of stone quarried on the island, it first opened in 1856 as a convict prison. That legacy had its effect. Portland Borstal was designed as the Colditz of the Borstal Service, where brutality was an everyday occurrence and the majority of staff appeared to have been chosen for their arrogance and physical size: bullies employed by the State.

I found out shortly after my arrival that this was a place where getting in trouble with the authorities was to be avoided if at all possible; but in my case it wasn't. I had heard a great deal about E Hall – the punishment block – but it had to be experienced to be believed. I was first placed in Grenville House and later moved to Nelson – all the houses in Portland were named after famous Admirals, the others being Rodney, Blake, Benbow and Hood.

One of the major faults of the Borstal Service was that it was founded on a philosophy that you could cure the criminal by discipline, hard work and skills training; it was a flawed philosophy. At Portland there were many vocational courses, ranging from motor mechanics to bricklaying, and the education department ran day and evening classes in academic subjects catering for all levels from remedial to degree; the pass rates were extremely high, but so too were the reconviction rates of those who took part. The philosophy was flawed in that it did not address the 'offending behaviour' which brought the person to the bortsal in the first place. It is no use training a prisoner to be a bricklayer if you do not train the bricklayer not to burgle houses – he is there because he burgles houses not because he can't build the damn things. We have to get our penal policy the right way around: reform the offending behaviour and then utilise the skills training, that is the way forward.

I had been at Portland just a few weeks when I was forced to pay my first visit to E Hall, the punishment block I had heard so much about. It is an old two-storey building with a courtyard on each side. The cells are tiny and contain a genuine tree stump bolted to the floor for a chair. The table is a piece of wooden planking fixed into one corner of the wall, while the bed is a small concrete platform raised six inches from the floor; you didn't sleep on the concrete, they gave you a wooden bed board for that.

The bed board was carried out of the cell at 6 a.m. every day and given back at 8 p.m. along with sheets and blankets. At 6.30 a.m. all trainees under punishment would stand by their doors and the shout would go out for 'Exercise!'. We would then move to the courtyard and, in shorts and vest, go through a hectic half-hour of physical training. This was carried out seven days of the week, irrespective of the weather. The session would be completed with a three-length swim of the open-air pool, which at that time of the day was bitterly cold. I do not recall that Portland ever did anything to address my offending behaviour, but I certainly outran a large number of policemen on my release.

After the PE session was over we were marched – and I mean *marched* – back to the block where we ate breakfast locked alone in our cells. During the morning we spent our time scrubbing out the cell with wire wool and if the staff were in a good mood they'd throw in a metal bin to clean just to ease the boredom. There was strictly no speaking and a roll-up was out of the question. The governor conducted his rounds each morning and you had to stand at your door and march forward giving your name and number. Each afternoon we would all move into the courtyard where we would spend three hours sawing logs with a huge double-handed saw. Many people down in the block were not sent there for a specified time but were known as RFHUFO – Removed From House Until Further Orders. I knew one boy who spent his whole sentence down there because he would not give in, though ten days was the average stretch and they rarely returned for a second dose. I spent eighty-seven days down the block, but I was always a slow learner!

When I left Portland Borstal – directly from the block and still wearing the 'shiner' that my refusal to scrub out my cell on my last day had earned me – I went once again to the Portsmouth area. My probation officer had arranged accommodation for me and told me to come and see him 'in a month or so'; it was six weeks before I made it to the dock of the local magistrates' court. I had been released from Portland Borstal on 29 June 1976 – on 2 August I was sentenced to six months' imprisonment for burglary of a hotel and theft of a suitcase in Salisbury – an 'open-and-shut case' as the laughing policeman in the dock put it. A few hours later, as I was seated in the police van taking me from the court to Winchester Prison, I had already decided that I was going to be a Mormon.

PART TWO

How Men Their Brothers Maim

As a 'young offender' I was what you might call a semi-skilled criminal; halfway between the reformable borstal trainee and the recidivist prison convict. I had not been in Winchester prison very long when I was carted down the block and placed on report for being abusive to staff who were dishing out the midday meal. The food at Winchester at that time was appalling: frequently cold, always uninviting and dished up on trays which had seen better days and not enough soap and water – and it has not improved to any great degree since.

Food in prison is always a major cause of complaint. There are very few prisons where the food is decent – Cardiff prison is one of the exceptions. Prison kitchens enjoy Crown immunity from prosecution and, until recently, environmental health officers had no right of entry. Those who dispute the dreadful state of prison kitchens should pick up any of the annual reports of HM Chief Inspector of Prisons and see the scathing remarks which he continues to make year after year.

For being abusive to his officers, the governor of Winchester gave me three days cellular confinement in the punishment block. I enjoyed the solitude and the three days were soon over. When two officers opened my door on the morning of my third day and told me to go back up to the wing, they were not impressed with my refusal to leave. In the punishment block I was better off than many of my friends on the landings above me. I had a cell to myself, whereas they had to share, and I had peace and quiet instead of noise and hassle; you soon begin to appreciate such things in prison.

Prison officers tend to be very discipline-minded; orders are orders and they take on a significance not far short of the Ten Commandments. If the governor had ordered that a man had to leave the punishment block, then he had to leave – 'You can't refuse to move,' as they innocently put it. That they would not hesitate to bring me back down the block once I was on the wing and had committed another offence did not appear to have dawned on them. An impasse had been reached. They demanded with all the rigidity of their office that I leave the block, and I in turn demanded that I stay put. They began physically to pull me out of the cell, but I held on to the pipes. When they snatched my hands off the pipes, I grabbed hold of the bed. When they removed me from the bed, I grabbed for the pipes again. The whole thing began to take on a comical aspect until in desperation one of them shouted 'Fuck it, just leave him,' and they went out and closed the door and left me in peace.

My six-month sentence passed by rather peacefully after that. I enjoyed my solitude and spent my time exercising in the cell or shouting out of the window to my pals on the wing upstairs. The effect of the solitary was that I was becoming more and more subversive. Prison officers who came to my door to slop out or to take me on exercise were met with a torrent of abuse and their attempts to calm me failed completely. Contact with my family was non-existent except that my dad continued to come and visit me. My brother Bill had made it clear that I was 'nothing but an embarrassment' to him, while Kathy, who was by this time married with a young son called Matthew, also made it clear that she wanted nothing to do with me. Yvonne was somewhere in the distance, while my two stepsisters had long since broken away from everyone after the death of my mother and wanted nothing to do with any of us – what a family!

I left Winchester prison on the morning of 8 November 1976, one month after my nineteenth birthday, and returned to Portsmouth. I was a complete arsehole, out to do as much damage as I could and would not stand anyone being in control of me. I hated authority in all its various guises. I was selfish beyond belief and did not have many friends; those I had never remained around for long, and I don't blame them – I hated me too.

I was a product of the system in all senses of the word. I had no time for others and was concerned with myself alone. While out of prison this time I was a thoroughly mixed-up person. I didn't know if I was gay or straight and my sexual emotions were difficult to understand. I did have a few girlfriends and at one time became very attached to a lovely girl called Jill, but the relationship was destined to be short-lived.

I found the pressures of existence outside of prison difficult to handle; this world of freedom was so alien to me. I was not used to making decisions and could not handle the pressure that accompanied them. Many times at night, in the loneliness of my bedsit, I would yearn to be back inside; I could cope there, I knew where I stood and what I was supposed to do – even if I very rarely did it.

On 24 January 1977 I appeared before His Honour Judge Ian Starforth-Hill at the Salisbury Crown Court; he was at that time a man not known for his leniency, though he appears to have mellowed during the years since then. I had been arrested for burglary of a hotel and stealing food out of the kitchen. I had just a few pounds dole money to live on, and no experience of making ends meet in an honest way. The hotel had food, I needed it and so I took it; justifying it on the basis that they could do without it, whereas I couldn't. The judge was not impressed with my record but I think he recognised that concealed behind all the hatred there was a fundamental problem that had to be dealt with. He attempted to discover the root cause by remanding me to Winchester prison for medical reports. Four weeks later, when I returned to the court for sentencing, I was given a two-year probation order with a condition of residence at St James Hospital in Portsmouth, an open psychiatric clinic.

My then probation officer, David Bradshaw, one of the few probation officers I've met who has a genuine interest in his charges, drove me to the hospital from the court and we arrived there in the early evening. I was very apprehensive about the place, convinced that it was only one step away from Broadmoor, and so I arrived with all the wrong attitudes – and kept them for the short time I was there. There were no walls, no screws, no fences, no cells, in fact nothing to keep me in at all; I lasted six weeks before the police were called to take me away.

I had been staying out all night and the doctors had had quite enough of this man who came in only to eat his meals and wanted no part in their 'silly psychiatric discussions'. I found myself once more in front of Starforth-Hill and it did not bode well – I was sentenced to three years.

Within a few months I was 'starred-up', that is, officially made into an adult prisoner. This should not happen until the person has reached twenty-one but it is common practice to make young offenders who represent a management and control problem into adults in the hope that the adult prison system will cure them of their subversiveness. For me, and typically, it only made it worse. I was first sent to Wormwood Scrubs where I was placed in a three-man cell on C Wing, at that time the allocation wing where prisoners are security classified and then allocated to an appropriate prison, a process which takes many months to complete.

When the governor of Wormwood Scrubs, John McCarthy, wrote his famous letter to *The Times* in 1981, describing his prison as a 'penal dustbin', he was being quite modest; the conditions were appalling. I made an application to see the prison's Board of Visitors (BOV) to complain about the inhumanity of the place – it was two and a half months before I was taken to see them at 2 p.m. one day.

I was taken out of my cell, searched, and escorted to the administration block where I was placed in a waiting room and told I would be seen 'shortly'. One hour and fifty minutes later I was shown into the board room and found myself facing a large horseshoe table around the outside of which were seated the twenty-five members of the BOV, along with the governor and his deputy – and two uniformed prison officers. The board were discussing the requirement for a new roof for the Officers' Social Club and I was given a chair and told to be quiet.

As I looked around the room, I found myself in the company of middle-aged, middle-class professionals, with la-di-da accents. In Savile Row suits or Yves St-Laurent dresses, they all looked neatly turned out. As I sat and waited for their discussions to end, watching them drinking coffee from bone-china cups brought in by a secretary, I looked around the brightly decorated room. Oil paintings graced the walls, one of a storm at sea and another of the front of the prison, flowers bloomed in a vase in one corner, and crushed-velvet curtains went all the way from ceiling to floor. Only fifty yards from where I sat, men were locked up twenty-three hours a day in dreadful conditions. As the talking finally came to an end and a few members took the opportunity to refill their cups with coffee, I was struck by the distance that separated our lifestyles. I wasn't trying to make prisons a place of luxury, only to get what were the everyday basics for decent human living: the hot bath and the clean clothes, access to sanitation and reasonable food served on clean trays. What I sought was humanity.

When I was finally invited to speak, I said that I wished to complain about the conditions in which I was housed. I explained that I was locked in a cell with two others for twenty-three hours a day. There was one piss-pot between the three of us, and that didn't have a lid. We had no lockers in which to store our clothing, and the cell, situated next to the ablutions, was overrun with cockroaches. The prison yard outside the cell, I complained, was awash with human excreta where prisoners had thrown their bodily waste out of the window rather than live with it for sixteen hours a day. I was permitted one bath a week in a communal bath-house whose roof was open to the sky and through which pigeons fluttered in and out or stood perched on the tiles intent upon discharge. I was allowed one change of clothes per week, and the bed in my cell had a mattress with a hole in a suspicious place while the blankets had not seen the inside of a washing machine for at least a year.

In all I spoke for about ten minutes before the chairman cut me short and informed me that my complaints had been noted and that they would get back to me 'shortly'. I was ushered out of the room, searched again in case I'd seen fit to remove anything, and then returned to my cell. Though I remained in that prison for the next nine months I was seen by the BOV on only one further occasion and, as I shall tell you later, it wasn't to discuss the issue of socks or piss-pot lids.

Three months after my arrival I was given a job in the prison kitchen and only came back to the wing at night to fall exhausted into my bed. A few weeks after I started in the kitchen I was awoken early one Monday morning by two prison officers who informed me that I was being taken to the block as I had been placed on report. They served me with a charge sheet which alleged that I had 'offended against Good Order and Discipline by laughing and joking in the prison chapel' the day before. I knew they had the wrong man; I'd been at work in the kitchen the day before, and hadn't been inside a church since my mother's funeral.

The notice of report – charge sheet – they gave me stated that I could, if I so wished, make my defence to the charge in writing on the reverse side of the form. In the quiet of the punishment block I picked up my pen and began to write, confident that I could show I had done nothing wrong. This was my first nicking in the adult prison system, which operates under different rules from the young offender institutions, and it was to be an eye-opener.

A few hours later I was marched into the adjudication room to face the governor. He was seated behind his desk busily writing as he completed the paperwork of the case before mine. As he finished writing he very slowly raised his head and his eyes travelled up from my shoes until they reached my waist, then he threw down his pen, pointed his finger at me and screamed, 'Get your fucking hands out of your pockets!' I could have made a better first impression. The governor had quite a repertoire of expletives and for the next few minutes he ran through some of them, ending by asking if I thought his adjudication room was 'a fucking betting shop'.

I stood in front of him, with my hands now by my sides, and listened as the reporting officer gave his evidence. He had been on duty in the chapel when he had had to speak to an inmate who was creating a disturbance by laughing and joking; according to him, that inmate was me. I handed in my neatly written defence in which I asked to call the kitchen officer to support my case that I had not been near the chapel the day before and had actually been hard at work. The governor picked it up, perused it, and then threw it into the bin by his right foot, issuing a one-word verdict: 'Bollocks'.

He slipped his half-moon glasses to the end of his nose and, looking me right in the eyes, said, 'Officers at Wormwood Scrubs do not tell lies. If they tell me you have been seen riding a motorbike around the fucking exercise yard, then I want to know where you got the petrol.' His raised hand stopped the intended interjection in my throat. 'I have only two things to say to you. The first is twenty-eight days' loss of remission and the second is get the fuck out of my adjudication room.' With that I was spun round and manhandled back to my place of work in the kitchen. I felt a burning sense of grievance at the extra month which, in less than five minutes, had just been added to my sentence. That is the prison disciplinary system in action and I shall come back to it again later.

Prison kitchens are a hive of underground activity. It may not look like a great deal is going on, but under the surface is a whole world of subterfuge, deception and downright theft taking place before your very eyes. Prices are quoted, orders are taken and goods are delivered often within the hour; Tesco couldn't match that for service.

D Hall in Wormwood Scrubs is reserved mainly for life-sentence prisoners. When full, which is more the rule than the exception, it holds in excess of 400 and it is a thoroughly depressing place in which to be confined. It is a large, rambling Victorian relic of a bygone era, typical of our life-sentence system – another subject I'll come to later. D Hall at that time was the only wing in the prison which had its own cooking facilities in the recreation area; as a consequence there was a huge trade in the foodstuffs that were intended for the D Hall pots.

Meat delivery came on a Thursday and the lorry would back up to the kitchen doors, where the prisoners who worked in the kitchen would lift and shift the meat into the huge walk-in freezer no more than 15 yards away. In that distance – often with a number of catering officers trying to watch what was happening – a lamb could lose all four legs, and I've seen pigs not only fly through the air, but then completely disappear! Chickens too were highly sought after and the frozen variety would whizz through the air at far greater speed than they ever flew through it when they were alive. Cheese, eggs, sausages, tomatoes, tea, coffee, milk, sugar, bread, butter . . . the list was endless. I once saw a lad knocked unconscious, quite by accident, when he was hit right between the eyes by a piece of frozen fish which was, or would have been, on its way to the D Hall pot.

One day a bald-headed officer, known throughout Wormwood Scrubs as Mudguard – because, as it was explained to me, 'he's shiny on top, but full of shit underneath' – was sent to work in the kitchen as a relief catering officer; he had been in the Army Catering Corps prior to joining the

Prison Service a few months before. He was shown the way to the staff changing room and was given a set of whites to wear. Later in the morning he returned to the changing room to find that not only had his cigarettes and lighter been lifted, but his leather jacket had also disappeared. The final straw was to discover that the sign saying Staff Changing Room had by then been replaced with its correct notice – Inmates' Rest Room.

I did not take the property but as I was the one who showed him to the room in the first place he was, perhaps understandably, convinced that it was me. They turned the kitchen upside down, and while they discovered ten gallons of illicit hooch merrily bubbling away in the vegetable store, the jacket, cigarettes and lighter were nowhere to be seen. I doubt that he ever did get his jacket back, since it had been smuggled to D Hall during the morning, sold to the highest bidder, and then slipped into the reception and placed in the private-property box of its new owner the same afternoon – c'est la vie!

I was sacked from my position as copperman ('coppers' being huge steam-driven cooking pots stirred with a paddle the size of a boating oar) for the heinous offence of purloining sugar from the custard mix a week or so after the incident with the jacket; an offence which cost me another visit to the governor and a further fourteen days' loss of remission. Kitchen workers are usually kept together on the lower landing so as not to create havoc when they get up early in the morning for work. Because I had lost my job I had to change landings and, when I discovered my new landing officer was none other than Mudguard, I knew trouble lay just around the corner.

I found myself new employment in the education department where the education officer had a degree in law and had arranged law classes each week, taught by a junior barrister from the Temple, Mr Adu. I enrolled and was at once captivated by the subject. I studied every single day and long into the nights. As the education officer put it, 'Mark, if you want to play the game and fight the system, you first have to learn the rules.' I threw myself into legal studies with all the energy I possessed. I read book after book, and spent hours in the education office discussing abstract legal points; within six months I was well on my way to an A level in law, which I passed a short time later – and the Home Office have regretted it ever since.

Things came to a head between Mudguard and myself after just a few months in which we had both shot across each other's bows: he couldn't resist picking me up for the slightest little thing, and I couldn't resist asking whether he'd got a light or seen a leather jacket hanging around. In effect it was doing neither of us any good and we should have known better – but in prison you become bored with too little activity and we continued to play the baiting game.

One evening, when I came back from the servery on the ground floor after collecting my tea, I found Mudguard outside my cell with a suspicious grin on his face. As he closed the door he winked and bade me a good night as he went on his way; the alarm bells were ringing in my head before he'd gone three steps. I searched the cell convinced that he'd planted something and was on his way back to 'spin' me (to search my cell) at any moment. I eventually discovered his handiwork at 10 p.m. As I went to climb into bed, I found he'd emptied the contents of a piss-pot into it.

When Mudguard opened my door in the morning, I dived out of bed and tackled him verbally about it. Of course, being a courageous sort of chap, he denied it, but we both knew he'd done it. As I stood at the cell door in my underpants giving him abuse, he fell into his prison officer mode, casually throwing a piece of advice in my direction: 'If you've got a complaint, put it in writing.' 'That,' I shouted, 'would be a total waste of time as you can't fucking read!'

It was not the piss that annoyed me. By then I had long grown used to the depths to which people in prison are forced to sink. I was annoyed because I'd not taken precautions to prevent it from happening. From then on, whenever he was on the landing and I was out of the cell, there was always someone looking; it cost me a quarter ounce of tobacco a week, but it was worth it for a good night's sleep.

After a bit of thought, but not a lot, I decided that I would put in a complaint and so I applied to see the wing governor. I was told that if I wished to proceed, I should write out a full statement of complaint and hand it in for investigation, which I did. The governor assured me that he would get back to me soon and, true to his word, he did – placing me on a disciplinary charge for making a 'false and malicious allegation' against Mudguard – so much for going through the proper channels!

I appeared before the prison governor charged with the offence and was informed that because of 'its nature and gravity' he was refusing to deal with it. 'My powers of punishment are quite inadequate for this,' he told me. The case was therefore remanded for hearing by the prison's BOV, the second time I was to meet them.

There have been BOVs in our prisons since the Prison Act 1898, when they were created for non-local prisons. Local prisons already had Visiting Committees, elected by magistrates at the local quarter sessions. Following the abolition of quarter sessions by the Courts Act 1971, BOVs were appointed to replace the Visiting Committees; currently there are some 1700 members in post, dispersed around every prison in England and Wales. The reason for their creation was to inject into the penal system some degree of independent scrutiny; whether that has been achieved depends on which side of the cell door you happen to be.

In theory the BOV is an independent body which should command the respect of both prisoners and prison officers alike. Sir George Waller, giving judgement in the Court of Appeal in 1978, remarked, 'A Board of Visitors holds the balance between the Governor and the internal discipline of the prison and the prisoner himself, and when sitting can be regarded as an impartial and independent authority.' But prisoners mistrust them, seeing them as no more than an extension of the prison governor, a chameleon device conveniently used for rubber-stamping his decisions and legitimising his actions; and in their disciplinary capacity they have a dreadful reputation in the courts.

In cases that have come before the High Court for judicial review of disciplinary decisions, judges have found Boards refusing to allow defence witnesses to be called, misapplying the law, fettering their discretion to grant legal representation, preventing officers who report offences from being cross-examined, allowing prejudicial inadmissible evidence to be used, insisting on finding guilt in at least two cases where the High Court ruled no offence had been committed and, astonishingly for a body that seeks to be seen as independent, even ordering that a prisoner be placed on a charge when they have no legal authority to do so. Given such circumstances, is it really so surprising that faith in their 'independence', and in the Prison Disciplinary System (PDS) itself, has simply failed to develop?

> Said Alice, 'That's not a regular rule, you invented it just now.'
> 'It's the oldest rule in the book,' said the King.
> (Lewis Carroll, *Alice in Wonderland*)

Like the main criminal justice system, the PDS is a two-tier structure. Prison governors hear the majority of charges – some 80,000 per year – and, with their limited powers of punishment, they equate to the magistrates' court. In some 3000 cases a year, where prison governors feel their powers of punishment are inadequate, they refer the case to 'crown court' of the PDS: the prison's BOV. BOVs have quite substantial disciplinary sanctions at their disposal and are neither afraid nor reluctant to use them.

56

Until recently the various Offences against Discipline set out in Rule 47 of the Prison Rules 1964 (SI.388/64) fell into three distinct categories: Governors' Offences, Graver Offences and Especially Grave Offences. On 1 April 1989 those divisions were swept away by enactment of the Prison Rules (Amendment) 1989 (SI.330/89). As referral to the BOV, with its increased powers of punishment, previously depended to a very large extent on the category of the offence, the consequence of sweeping away those divisions has been to invest prison governors with absolute and unfettered discretion as to which charges they refer to the second tier. The criterion for referral, for all offences against discipline, is now stated as the governor being satisfied that 'in the nature and circumstances of the offence, his own powers of punishment are inadequate'.

The new system was initially conceived following the successes in the High Court five years previously in 1984 when a large number of prisoners had their BOV disciplinary adjudications (stemming from the riots at Albany and Wormwood Scrubs prisons) quashed by the High Court because of failure to apply the law and act fairly. That case, *R. v. Secretary of State, ex.p Tarrant et al.* ([1984] 1 All ER 799), led directly to the establishment of the Prior Committee to inquire into the PDS and, subsequently, to the amendment of the Prison Rules.

The new disciplinary rules of April 1989 to some extent incorporated the scathing criticism which had flowed from the courts in the previous fifteen years. The new system abolished the offence I was then facing, of making a false and malicious allegation against an officer, as well as that of repeatedly making groundless complaints. The offences of Mutiny and Incitement to Mutiny were also abolished, though following the riots that hit the penal system in April 1990 the Home Secretary has now taken steps to create a new criminal offence of 'prison mutiny', which carries a maximum sentence of ten years' imprisonment – and it is mandatory that such a sentence be served consecutively to the one being served at the time of the offence.

The 'new' Rule 47 sets out the offences against discipline in twenty-two numbered paragraphs:

1 Commits any assault;

2 Detains any person against his will;

3 Denies access to any part of the prison to any officer;

4 Fights with any person;

5 Intentionally endangers the health or personal safety of others or, by his conduct, is reckless whether such health and personal safety is endangered;

6 Intentionally obstructs an officer in the execution of his duty;

7 Escapes or absconds from prison or from legal custody;

8 Fails –
   a. to return when he should return after being temporarily released under Rule 6 of these Rules, or
   b. to comply with any condition upon which he is so released;

9 Has in his possession –
   a. any unauthorised article, or
   b. a greater quantity of any article than he is authorised to have;

10 Sells or delivers to any person any unauthorised article;

11 Sells or without permission delivers to any person any article he is allowed to have only for his own use;

12 Takes improperly any article belonging to another person or to a prison;

13 Intentionally or recklessly sets fire to any part of a prison or any property, whether or not his own;

14 Destroys or damages any part of the prison or any other property, other than his own;

15 Absents himself from any place where he is required to be or is present at any place where he is not authorised to be;

16 Is disrespectful to any officer or any person visiting a prison;

17 Uses threatening, abusive or insulting words or behaviour;

18 Intentionally fails to work properly or being required to work refuses to do so;

19 Disobeys any lawful order;

20 Disobeys or fails to comply with any rule or regulation applying to him;

21 In any way offends against Good Order and Discipline;

22 a. Attempts to commit,
   b. Incites another prisoner to commit;
   c. Assists another prisoner to commit or attempt to commit, any of the foregoing offences.

And let's see you get out of that in a hurry!

Prison Rule 48 requires that the prisoner must be charged 'as soon as possible', and, unless in exceptional circumstances, within forty-eight hours of the discovery of the offence. Once a prisoner has been charged he is generally held in the punishment block and from that point on he is unable to have any contact with others. He cannot collect evidence or speak to witnesses who may have seen what happened, nor is he given any real details of the case he has to meet. The charge sheet will set out brief details of the alleged offence, but it does not include details of any other evidence that may be called against him.

There is no limit on how long a prisoner may remain segregated down the punishment block awaiting adjudication. The case must be opened within twenty-four hours of the charge being made – except where that includes a Sunday or public holiday – but it can then be adjourned for months while police or forensic examinations take place. There is no mechanism for reviewing the need to keep the person in segregation while the various investigations are being carried out. I once spent four and a half months locked in segregation awaiting an adjudication, only to have the case dismissed when it finally came to 'trial'. To quote again from *Alice in Wonderland*: 'Sentence first, verdict last.'

At a disciplinary adjudication, there is a laid-down procedure which should be followed, but rarely is. The prisoner stands at one end of a long T-shaped table facing the governor or BOV. In front, with their backs to the 'court', stand two prison officers; with hands on balls and heads bowed, they stand with their noses no more than three inches from your own. This practice of eye-balling has been condemned by the courts and the Home Office has issued instructions that it must not continue; most rules such as this one are ignored.

Once the charge has been read and the plea taken, the hearing does not take long. Essentially it's a matter of the officer giving his evidence, the prisoner disputing it and the governor or BOV finding the charge proved; followed rather rapidly by sentence. Before we return to the case of the 'false and malicious allegation' against Mudguard at Wormwood Scrubs, it is worth looking at the powers of punishment which are now set out in the new Rules. Essentially it depends on whether the sentence is passed by the governor or the BOV (who were finally stripped of all their disciplinary powers on 1 April 1992 – and not before time).

Rule 50.

1   If [the governor] finds a prisoner guilty of an offence against discipline, the governor may . . . impose one or more of the following punishments:

   a.   Caution;

   b.   Forfeiture for a period not exceeding 28 days of any of the privileges under Rule 4 of these Rules (BOV: unlimited period);

   c.   Exclusion from associated work for a period not exceeding 14 days (BOV: 56 days);

d. Stoppage of earnings for a period not exceeding 28 days (BOV: 56 days).

e. Cellular confinement for a period not exceeding 3 days (BOV: 56 days);

f. Forfeiture of remission of sentence for a period not exceeding 28 days (BOV: 120 days per charge, subject to a limit of 180 days per adjudication);

g. In the case of a prisoner otherwise entitled to them [books, newspapers etc.], forfeiture for any period of the right under Rule 41(1) of these Rules to have the articles there mentioned (BOV: ditto);

h. In the case of a prisoner guilty of escaping or attempting to escape and who is entitled to it, forfeiture of the right to wear his own clothes under Rule 20 (1) of these Rules (BOV: ditto).

There were three people facing me down the T-shaped table as I entered the BOV adjudication room at Wormwood Scrubs, one afternoon in March 1977. The elderly chairman in the centre was flanked on each side by a female member of the Board. Mudguard was present, of course, to see that his maliciously defamed reputation was restored to its former glory, and the security principal officer acted as the governor's prosecutor.

The security officer began by informing the Board that the governor had already investigated the complaint and found that it was both false and malicious – and effectively managed to put it across in such a way as to leave them no choice but to support him. When he had completed his case, which took all of three minutes, I noticed that he slipped a piece of paper to the chairman, muttering something about it being 'from the governor'. The Board read the paper and then pushed it to one side; I was, to say the least, intrigued.

When I asked what the letter's contents were, I was informed by the chairman that it was a 'personal communication' to them from the governor. Here they were, discussing a serious allegation in which my liberty was at stake and, not being content with the under-the-table investigations, they now wanted to have private notes flying around the place – well, we'd see about that! I rose up on my legal hind legs and with all the A-level law I could muster gave them a lecture on procedural fairness. I formally asked the Board for access to the contents of the letter and they, with equal formality, refused. I pressed the issue for ten minutes, quoting supporting cases they'd never heard of – and neither had I until I created them and their supporting 'precedents' moments earlier. In the end they gave ground, agreeing to read it out, but they wouldn't let me near it.

The letter was indeed from the governor, the man who had investigated the case and was responsible for my present predicament. He now informed the Board that I was a 'subversive, devious and disruptive prisoner who has made these types of false and malicious allegations in the past'; an illuminating piece of reporting, if only for the fact that it was untrue – well, at least the last bit.

I informed them that the letter from the governor was, 'in my respectful submission', wholly unfair at this stage of the proceedings, when they had not yet reached a decision as to guilt. The chairman began to look worried, and told me that while the Board had read the document, they would pay no attention to it. I responded by saying that they could hardly forget something they had read only moments ago, but I left the matter there: my objection had been noted on the transcript of the hearing and that was the important point.

I was denied permission to call defence witnesses on the grounds that it would disrupt the prison workshops, and when I asked to cross-examine Mudguard the Board allowed a few questions but cut me short whenever I got close to showing that the allegation, far from being false and malicious, was in fact completely accurate. I was, of course, found guilty and sentenced to a further thirty-five days imprisonment by way of lost remission. I was taken back to my cell and was poring over the chapters of De Smith's *Constitutional and Administrative Law* even before the door closed; it became clear as I read that it would not be an easy case to win.

There was little doubt that the letter from the governor to the BOV had been highly prejudicial and should not have been placed before them, but I realised also that there was a potential problem with my argument because of what lawyers call de bene esse evidence. Judges – and indeed magistrates in their examining capacity – sometimes have to hear de bene esse evidence, that is, evidence which is prejudicial to an accused, in order to decide upon its admissibility. Having heard it and decided that the evidence is inadmissible, they then have to attempt the rather difficult task of putting it from their minds as if they had never heard it. The law was quite clear that, on such occasions, knowledge of the inadmissible evidence could not give rise to a complaint that there had been a breach of natural justice.

However, to my way of thinking, this situation was slightly different. What was before the Board on this occasion was not, for example, a statement of an inadmissible confession to the 'crime', but what amounted to a signed list of previous convictions before they had determined whether I was guilty. It was a narrow distinction, but I felt it to be a worthy one. I decided to ask the High Court to quash the thirty-five days loss of remission, on the grounds of procedural impropriety. With one problem out of the way, I was then brought face to face with another.

The law in relation to prison disciplinary proceedings was at that time in a state of considerable flux. Following a riot at Hull Prison, in August and September 1976, the BOV from the prison toured the country adjudicating upon those who were charged with offences in relation to the riot; they ordered almost ninety years of remission to be forfeited. Their procedure was flawed, they misapplied the law and were biased beyond belief. A number of prisoners, inspired by the Canadian, Ronald St Germain, decided to challenge them in the High Court; it was to be a landmark case.

This was the first time that prisoners had ever sought to challenge the PDS in the courts and it was to herald a decade in which the injustices of the disciplinary system were revealed and to a large extent remedied; it ended with my own case in the House of Lords against the deputy governor of Parkhurst. When the case of *St Germain* came before the High Court the prisoners were defeated because the Lord Chief Justice decided that it would not be proper for the courts to become involved with internal prison discipline. Moreover, feared Lord Widgery, if BOV adjudications could be challenged in the courts by 'disgruntled prisoners', then why not prison governors' adjudications also? It was not a prospect he was prepared to tolerate.

Because of the decision in *St Germain*, it seemed that I was destined to fail, and so I contented myself with formally petitioning the Home Secretary asking him to quash the thirty-five days loss of remission on the grounds of unfairness. The Home Office was obviously delighted with the decision in *St Germain*, and the Home Secretary formally refused my petition a few weeks later in the full knowledge that, as the law stood, I had nowhere else to go. But the tide started to turn against the Home Office, the prisoners took the decision of the High Court to the Court of Appeal, and I waited each day for news of the decision.

On 3 October 1978 I was given the best twenty-first birthday present I could ever have received: the Court of Appeal reversed the decision in *St Germain* and held that the disciplinary decisions of a prison BOV were capable of being challenged in the courts – it was all systems go as I set about preparing the first of many subsequent visits to the High Court, armed with this wondrous new weapon I'd discovered called 'judicial review'.

I spent many hours planning the case and was given a good deal of advice by the barrister from the Temple who taught law at the Scrubs. The education officer was also assisting me, which did not go down at all well with the Wormwood Scrubs authorities. On 1 June 1979, while I was still waiting for the case to come before the High Court, I was informed one morning that I was being transferred to Maidstone Prison in Kent, and I arrived there four hours later.

Maidstone is known to be a liberal prison and much of its leniency was the result of the progressive regime created by its then governor, the Rev. Peter Timms. He is one of the very few prison governors for whom I have had the slightest degree of respect. However, my subversive attitude meant that we still came into conflict; something which I can now see, with the benefit of hindsight, was completely my own fault.

The date for the court case was drawing near. It had been listed for hearing on 11 August 1979 – thirty-five days before my date of release – and success would inevitably mean an immediate discharge. Because I could not get legal aid, and was not able to afford the £70 which the Home Office insisted they would charge me for the provision of prison transport, I could not attend the hearing. Instead I placed all of my arguments and legal submissions in a 56-page affidavit which I lodged at the court and served on the Treasury solicitor who was acting for the Board of Visitors.

When 11 August finally dawned, I was up at 6 a.m. and spent the whole of the day on tenterhooks waiting for news. By the time dinner had come and gone and tea had arrived, I was devastated by the belief that I'd lost. But, ten minutes after my cell door had been closed, it was reopened by a screw who spoke the words I'd been waiting to hear all day: 'You've won, pack your kit, you're going home.'

In the prison reception they asked me where I wanted to go so they could fill out the travel warrant, and in my excitement I said Plymouth instead of Portsmouth, with the result that in the early hours of the following morning I found myself wandering down Union Street – known in Plymouth as the Strip. I found lodgings in a local guesthouse and got a driving licence in the name of Smith, with which I got my first job in the city, as an ambulanceman with the Devon Ambulance Service based at Greenbank. For the next five months I was driving around with blue lights flashing, sirens blaring and injured people in the back – and I hadn't even passed my driving test. At the end of five months I resigned from the Ambulance Service, certainly the most worthwhile job I've ever had, simply because I could not afford to live on the pittance that was paid for wages: for a forty-hour week and ten hours overtime, I collected £78.

I found my next job as a bus conductor with the Western National Bus Company in Plymouth. I have always liked meeting people and I quite enjoyed my time on the buses. The problem was that the job involved handling money and my fingers were still sticky. The fiddles were as numerous as they were well known. The common one was to corrupt the ticket. On the route I travelled the most common ticket cost 32p; but the trick was to issue a 2p ticket – 'in error' if anyone ever noticed – while the other 30p went into my pocket. I was always getting bollockings from the various inspectors who hid along the route, but they really blew a gasket the day I became so fed up with climbing up and down the stairs that I 'discovered' the stairs were dangerous and promptly closed off the top deck completely for the rest of the day! In the end I remedied the intrusion of the inspectors by paying the driver to sail right past them whenever they tried to stop the bus.

My sexual identity was still obscured because of past experiences, but I felt more and more that I was gay; it was something I felt guilty about, and I couldn't understand why I wasn't 'straight' like the other 'normal' people. At the garage where I was based was another conductor of my own age (22) and, I don't know how, but I knew he was gay – I'll call him Steve. He was looking for a flat of his own as he was still living at home, and he asked whether he could move in with me for a few weeks until he could find somewhere. I agreed, and that was the start of a relationship which lasted for the next three months.

I was 'happy' in one way during the few months Steve and I spent together, but I was also feeling uncomfortable about what I was doing. I was going through the phase that every gay person has to go through: am I or aren't I? It's a terrible dilemma to be faced with. Sexual relationships should be pleasurable and free from anxiety, but for me they were riddled with feelings of guilt which just about destroyed everything. At work we were just two 'straight' guys and that created pressures of its own, in addition to the ones we already had.

Steve told me one day that he had joined the TA and invited me to join too. I knew that I would have a problem with my criminal record, and he did not know about that. I went along one evening and took the plunge; either it would work out or it wouldn't. It didn't. I was called on another evening to the captain, who was flanked by a sergeant from the Ministry of Defence police. I was taken to a small room and interviewed about my record which they had, of course, discovered, despite my change of name. My position was quite clear: leave or be nicked. Though my life outside of prison was hard, I was not that eager to make a return so I left, pleased to be rid of all the bullshit that went with it.

That was also the end of the relationship with Steve, who could not understand why I hadn't told him of my record. He moved out and went back to live with his mother, leaving the bus depot a few weeks later; I haven't seen him since. With Steve back with his mother, I used to go out in the evenings by myself. Plymouth, being a major naval port, is full of nightclubs and Union Street was often full of fighting marines and sailors.

I met the person I shall call Rob in a nightclub in Plymouth, after he and I had been dumped on the pavement by the bouncers as a result of his fondness for playing football with the beer glasses. He was in the Navy, a year or two younger than me, and he moved into the flat about two weeks after we'd met on the concrete outside the nightclub. His moving in coincided with my losing my job on the buses. An inspector had become suspicious that a particular bus always seemed to sail past him as he sought to board it. He changed into civvies and mingled with the shoppers in the city centre. He was on the bus before I knew it, and the rest is history. I can still see his face asking why everyone on the bus appeared to be holding a 2p ticket! I got another job in a garage a few days later, running the car-audio boutique for a local main dealer; sales began to go down soon after I arrived.

One evening Rob and I paid a visit to the naval base and stole two walkie-talkies. Within twenty-four hours we were both under arrest. He was looking at detention quarters while for me I knew it meant prison. Rob's parents came down from South Wales for the court case, and watched as he was fined £440; I did not appear that day but was subsequently committed to the Crown Court for sentence. I met Rob's parents a number of times and we were close. They were caring people and I grew very attached to them. One day, while I was waiting for the case to come to court, I found my own dad on the doorstep of my flat, blind drunk and singing loudly. I haven't a clue how he traced me as we'd not had any contact for at least twelve months.

My father has always been around on the edges of my life, but occasionally disappears for a year or two. Usually when he turns up he is the worse for drink, but his heart is always firmly in the right place. We have all done things that we will regret to our grave and the time I stole £200 from my father counts as one of those; one of the very few crimes that I have felt guilty about. He was not very well when he came to Plymouth and I became more worried about him almost with every passing day. One night when he seemed really bad, and against his wishes, I called in the local doctor. The examination was brief. He was in a bad way, and he was sent to the Royal Naval

Hospital at Stonehouse where he remained for the next two months. When he went into hospital he gave me his money to keep safe – I spent it. I have often wanted to discuss that with him, not that there is much to be said, but each time I raise it, he always says, 'It's water under the bridge, son.' Dad, I love you.

When Dad came out of hospital I had already appeared before the Crown Court and was sentenced to two and a half years in prison. The judge was not at all impressed with my record and the letter I produced from my employers did not carry much weight either; which is probably not surprising, since I'd written it myself on paper I'd taken from the managing director's office. From the Crown Court in Plymouth I was taken to Exeter prison. The huge gates closed behind me once more. It was 7 June 1980 and I was twenty-two.

I had not been in Exeter very long when my cell door opened one afternoon and a screw handed me a telegram that had arrived at the prison gates earlier in the day. I can still see that telegram; I read its contents many times. It was from Rob's father and showed the deep feelings that he and his family had for me. 'You are family', it began. 'We will stand by you whatever.' For the next fifteen months they did precisely that, coming to visit me regularly, writing each week and offering me a place to live on my release. I was subsequently transferred from Exeter to Dartmoor prison, and Rob's parents were outside the gates at 6.30 a.m. when I was released from there on 2 November 1981.

Living with Rob's parents in South Wales started off very well. I was happy and soon found employment with an electronic company in Brynmawr, about ten miles from their home. Rob was married shortly before I left Dartmoor, and I don't think he took to the idea of me living with his parents. He was still in the Navy when I was released, though left after getting married and starting a family.

On the surface my life at that time was good, but inside I felt I was living a lie. I realised by now of course that I was gay, but I still struggled desperately with the internal conflict and raging emotions that ignited. I took girls out, and had sexual relationships with them, but each one was simply one more 'act' in a long line – it was not 'me'. I longed to come out of the proverbial closet, and I'm fairly certain now that it would have been accepted by Rob's parents, but I didn't have the courage then to tell them. I couldn't face the truth, and I feared their rejection.

The pressure that was building up inside me was soon to see me back in prison. I left the computer company in Brynmawr and found employment with a large chain of foodstores as a trainee manager. One day, while working in their store in Newport, I was given a severe dressing down in front of everyone after being caught smoking. The bollocking was over the top and the area manager must have known it. Later that night I destroyed his warehouse by setting fire to it. I did not feel in the least guilty; to my mind he had deserved it. I look back now and I'm absolutely astounded that I ever did it. I cannot fathom where my head was at, or what I hoped to attain apart from revenge; that someone could have been killed does not escape me either. The police investigated the fire and interviewed me, but I denied any knowledge of it and the matter rested there.

One evening I was at a friend's house not far from Rob's parents when I received a phone call from his mother asking me to come home because 'we've been burgled'. She was always one for playing practical jokes and I didn't believe her, but I made the trip round the corner anyway to find that she was right. The television and video had been stolen and I instantly felt all eyes were on me. I hadn't done it and I went to bed that night feeling really pissed off. Rob's father did all but accuse me of it, and it was clear to all what he was thinking. Over the next week our relationship began to crumble.

One day, while visiting the probation officer in the town centre – only Rob's father knew where I had gone – I was arrested by two police officers in connection with the burglary and locked in the police station overnight. They questioned me endlessly and I denied any knowledge of it, but they too were convinced I was guilty. Only Rob's mother had the courage and the faith to stand up and tell me that she didn't believe I had done it – and the truth was that I hadn't. But after being released from the police station the atmosphere at home was terrible. There was no way I could continue to live there and so I packed my things and moved out to Manchester. I was gutted.

I fell back into crime and during the course of the next few weeks did more travelling than I'd ever done in my life. In Manchester I hired a car and promptly sold it to a garage for £3000. With that I went to Jersey and found employment in a hotel on the seafront in St Helier. I was working as a kitchen porter in the hotel, but I soon discovered where the pass keys to the rooms were kept and one afternoon I went through a few and took cash, cheque books and cards along with some suitcases; I flew out of Jersey that afternoon. First I went to Liverpool, and then to the Isle of Man, where I remained for a fortnight before flying out to London. In London I stayed the night with a friend, cashed a few cheques for funds and the following morning flew to Amsterdam; it was to be an experience I had never had before.

Amsterdam is so liberal that you can do your own thing and no one bothers about you in the least. Different ways of life converge in Amsterdam and co-exist quite happily. The police are nothing at all like the Met, but if you cross them they are complete bastards. I stayed in the Hotel Anco in the red-light district and discovered cannabis. I had a number of identities and credit cards to fit them, and after two weeks in Amsterdam I went to Schiphol Airport and, using the credit card of a Mr McConnell, booked a flight to Montreal in Canada and flew out the same afternoon. I had only a British Visitor's Passport at the time and a number of visas in various names, but none was for Canada and I spent the flight working out my story for arrival. I needn't have bothered – you don't need a visa for Canada!

In Montreal I stayed at the Holiday Inn for a week and then flew to Toronto where I booked into a very plush hotel, the Royal York, in the centre. I was making my way by cheque books and credit cards and had so many different identities that I hardly knew who I was from day to day. After a week in Toronto I decided the time had come for some sunshine and, leaving with about a dozen cheque books and credit cards that I'd picked up during my stay, I flew out of Toronto for Bermuda. I had to fly via New York and, with no US visa, I had to remain in the custody of a New York immigration official because I was what they termed a Trove – in transit without visa. When I arrived in Bermuda the end of the line had almost come.

The pretty Bermudan girl behind the immigration desk asked me on my arrival for my passport and ticket, which I produced thinking I'd got it all sussed, but my planning had been flawed by a lack of information. I had only a single ticket to Bermuda and entry depends on the visitor being in possession of a return ticket. I didn't have cash on me, but I did have some in my case which I opened without realising that the person standing behind me was a plain-clothes policeman; his eyes bulged when he caught sight of the cheque books and very soon I found myself under arrest.

I was questioned for two hours and was just on my way to the local nick when some bright spark realised I hadn't been officially 'landed' in the country. The result was that I was sent first to New York, and then to Montreal where I spent a week in the immigration detention centre which occupied the top floor of a hotel and was quite luxurious. None of the rooms had doors and the officers used to sit in the corridor. There was no getting out of the place because all the windows were both barred and covered with steel grilles. I had an immigration hearing at the Guy Street headquarters and a few days later was deported to London – being excluded from Canada for twelve months.

On arrival back in London I was met off the plane by two members of the Greater Manchester Police and was taken to Moss Side police station for theft of the motor car I had hired and sold. I was soon on remand in Strangeways prison where my life was to continue its downward spiral.

Within prison sub-culture there is a distinct 'pecking order'. Armed robbery and offences of violence are pretty near the top when it comes to being invested with penal kudos, and the list then descends through drug dealers, burglars and credit-card 'kiters' until, at the bottom of the pile, you come to the hated child sex offenders; a group for whom I have always had an intense dislike, and probably with good reason. The majority of prisoners are just those who have dreamt of making the 'big one' and having enough money on which to live a life of luxury, but in reality have been incapable of success in even minor crime; and I was no different. We all constantly told the stories of great criminal successes, and with conviction, even though most of us knew they were all a pack of lies.

On the landing where I was in Strangeways in July 1982, was a man who, prison officers revealed, was a child sex offender. He was a housemaster in a local school and had been charged with gross indecency in relation to some of his pupils. He was a large man, and as a result either of courage or folly he refused to seek the protection of Rule 43 – where sexual offenders seek segregation in their own interests. One morning in the recess, while I was waiting to collect my water, he pushed in front of me and, without a word, drew his water and returned to his cell. The recess had gone very quiet. It is no excuse to say that what happened next was the result of me never being at my best first thing in the morning, or his own fault, or a combination of the two. I went back to my cell just as the landing screw was giving out the razor blades. He left two and went on his way. As soon as he had moved on, I took one of the blades and went to the cell of the nonce (sexual offender). He knew the truth was out the moment I pushed the door open, but I had the advantage of speed and surprise. I slashed him down the side of his face with the blade and went out of the cell leaving him on the floor holding his cheek together.

Had I been a little more intelligent and possessed more common sense, I would never have started out on that journey to his cell in the first place. Had I also been gifted with foresight I would have seen that not only did I stand very little chance of getting away with it, but that it would in fact lead directly to an appearance before Her Honour Judge Joanna Bracewell QC – and a five-year prison sentence. It's easy to be wise, as they say, after the event.

After the attack I was taken from my cell and placed in the punishment block on D1 landing where I made my first acquaintance with Norman Brown, the governor. At one time in his life he would have been a handsome man, but his face was now horribly disfigured with burns. He had served his country with distinction during the Second World War, and got blown out of the tank which he no doubt commanded with the same rigidity he brought to Strangeways. He wasn't a good governor by any stretch of the imagination, and in my view shares much of the responsibility for planting and cultivating the seeds which, a decade later, would bring the prison roof to the ground and a repair bill of twenty million pounds. The inmates cruelly referred to him as 'eighteen months' because 'he's only got an ear an' a half' while the staff all but walked in fear of him. Strangeways was Norman Brown's prison and people who didn't know it, soon found out.

While waiting in the punishment block for police investigations to be carried out I was kept in solitary confinement for the Good Order and Discipline of the prison. The block was a brutal place and I was assaulted by officers a number of times. Norman Brown insisted that inmates in the block did not use their beds during the day; the mattress had to be slipped down the side and the blankets folded into a box. The Home Office will tell you that prisoners in segregation for the Good Order and Discipline of the prison are not undergoing a punishment, but the regime operated by Norman Brown was little different to that.

I appeared before Judge Bracewell QC at the Manchester Crown Court on 8 October 1982 and following my sentencing was transferred from Manchester to the Long-Term Allocation Centre, then at Walton prison in Liverpool. I remained there for five months before being allocated to Long Lartin maximum-security prison, some two miles east of the village of South Littleton, near Evesham, in Worcestershire.

Long Lartin is the 'jewel' in the dispersal system of maximum-security prisons. The dispersal system was created in the late 1960s following a number of spectacular escapes by maximum-security prisoners: Charlie Wilson from Birmingham Prison in August 1964, Ronnie Biggs from Wandsworth Prison in July 1965, and George Blake, who apparently walked out of Wormwood Scrubs Prison in West London on a quiet autumn evening in October 1966. It was the Blake escape that resulted in the inquiry into prison security chaired by the late Earl Mountbatten. The Home Secretary acted on many of the recommendations set out in the Mountbatten Report, ordering, for example, that all prisoners be classified into one of four security categories: 'A' being maximum security through to 'D' which qualifies for open conditions. Mountbatten also recommended that all category A prisoners be located together in one purpose-built fortress-type prison on the Isle of Wight; he suggested the name Vectis.

The problems with a policy of concentration are obvious to anyone who knows the slightest thing about prisons, though they appear to have been overlooked in this case. If you have only one prison to house such prisoners, where do you hold them when that prison has been torn apart by a riot, and cannot be re-opened for the best part of a year? The Home Secretary placed the issue of long-term maximum-security prisoners with the Advisory Committee on the Penal System, chaired by then Cambridge criminologist, Professor Leon Radzinowicz. His committee took the opposite view to Mountbatten's and advocated a system of dispersal, in which the category A prisoners were dispersed around a small number of maximum-security prisons. Long Lartin prison, to which I was taken on 18 April 1983, was one of the eight dispersal prisons then in existence; today there are eleven.

Long Lartin was a very relaxed prison on the whole, successive governors taking the view that as the perimeter security was high, the regime inside the perimeter could be relaxed; a policy which was later reviewed and tightened in the wake of the successful helicopter escape from another dispersal prison (Gartree in Leicestershire) in December 1988. At Long Lartin I found myself mixing for the first time with sophisticated criminals, many of whom were serving long sentences which, in some cases, meant they would never be released.

I spoke to the so-called IRA terrorist, Gerard Conlon, of the Guildford Four, a number of times and was very pleased to have done so. I have no doubts that the quashing of the conviction was wholly correct, even though it took fifteen long years for the truth to emerge. Victory for Gerry, however, was only partial justice for the Conlon family. His father Giuseppe, one of the McGuire Seven, had his conviction finally quashed by the Court of Appeal ten years after he died in prison, still protesting his innocence. To paraphrase a columnist in the *Sunday Times*, the true test of justice is not by reference to the number of innocent men in prison, but to the speed and zeal with which they are released.

It was significant that in Long Lartin the IRA prisoners kept themselves very much to themselves and not once did I get the impression they considered Gerry Conlon one of their number. The recent and expensive outburst in the *Spectator* by the ageing Lord Denning, a man afflicted with an inability to remain impartial, has only served to add to the grave injustices which innocent men and women have already suffered – and anyone who doubts he has anti-Irish views should read his disgracefully worded and perversely argued judgement in the case of *Guilfoyle v. Home Office* ([1981] 1 QB 309).

While many of Lord Denning's judgements have been severely criticised over the years, the simple and disturbing fact is that despite the lessons of Guildford and Birmingham – not to mention the celebrated cases of the aptly named West Midlands Serious Crime Squad – far too many of our judges still refuse to accept the reality. Police officers do tell lies, and are more than capable of not only altering evidence but planting it too, as well as any one of a dozen other dubious practices that fall under the collective title of 'fitting 'em up'. We have been assured that, following the introduction of various safeguards in the Police and Criminal Evidence Act 1984 (PACE), the likes of the 'pub bombing' cases could not happen again, but that is simply not true. Where a person has been arrested under the provisions of the Prevention of Terrorism Act, PACE does not apply for the first forty-eight hours; every single one of the Guildford Four wrote what purported to be a 'confession' to the Guildford bombing within that period.

The haunting cases of the Guildford Four, Birmingham Six, McGuire Seven and Winchester Three revealed that twenty innocent people were locked up in our prisons for a decade and a half, while British justice scorned their pleas, turned a blind eye to their plight and where, at the end of the day, the Lord Chief Justice of England could not even find the humanity to utter one single word of apology. That the injustices in those cases have now been recognised and to some extent remedied should not mask the fact that we have fundamental problems with our legal system which urgently need to be tackled: equality before the law is the primary element of the rule of law, but it means little if you are presumed innocent only until proven Irish.

At Long Lartin, with its relaxed regime, it was fairly easy for me to become involved in legal studies. My A level in law qualified me for entry to the external law degree course of London University and I wrote away for details. The education officer was not too pleased when I popped my head around his door a week or so later and asked him if he had a spare £300. But it was the start of the new financial year, so I had timed it quite well, and I was subsequently registered with London University and tutored by Wolsey Hall in Oxford for the intermediate examinations which I passed the following year in June.

As 1983 progressed it became clear that in our new Home Secretary, Leon Brittan QC, we had a man who would make sweeping changes to the parole system. He made clear his view many times that there had to be a closer correlation between the sentence passed by the court and the time served in the prison. While the Court of Appeal, with its head in the clouds, claimed that judges do not take into account that a person may be eligible for parole, the fact remains that many judges do take account of it and sentence on precisely that basis. When Leon Brittan stood up at the Conservative Party conference on 11 October 1983, I was standing in a crowded television room in B Wing of Long Lartin waiting to hear the news; it was not good.

Leon Brittan gave notice that all prisoners who were serving five years or more for offences of drugs, sex or violence would not normally be granted parole, 'except in circumstances which are wholly exceptional', until the final few months of their sentence. Life-sentence prisoners who were convicted of murder during the course of a robbery, or the murder of police or prison officers, could expect to spend at least twenty years in prison, 'and for some a longer period may be necessary'. At a stroke the Home Secretary usurped the trial judge who had sentenced on the basis of the parole policy in force at the time, made parole reports in the future almost superfluous and, for the first time, united prisoners and prison officers alike.

During the course of the following few weeks, demonstrations in the prison were numerous. Work strikes took place not only in Long Lartin, but in other long-term dispersal prisons up and down the country. Television rooms, recreation areas and

78

exercise yards became places of sit-down protest and a number of screws were injured in the process. The common thread running through all these protests was simply that the new parole policy should not be made retrospective; it should apply, if at all, only to those sentenced after the date it came into effect. No one knew whether they would be included in the parole policy or what, if anything apart from imminent death, amounted to 'wholly exceptional' circumstances.

Like others I too was in limbo. My parole was due four months later and I had already filled out my representations and handed them in. I asked the governor, chairman of the Board of Visitors, regional director and anyone who would listen whether I came within the new parole policy or not; no one could tell me. I petitioned the Home Office, Parliament and even the Queen with the same question, all to no avail. I hated this penal system and all that it stood for. They treated you as no more than a number on a card to be rewritten and moved from slot to slot as they liked. I hated their double standards and illogical rules. I despised their physical abuse and frequent breaches of the few 'rights' I possessed. I was utterly committed to doing anything in my power to rectify all these; when injustice becomes the rule, resistance becomes the duty.

Two weeks before Christmas 1983 I was asked if I would like to go on the roof of the prison in protest at the new parole policy. I jumped at the chance. Getting up there, never mind staying up there, proved difficult, however. Michael and Vincent Hickey, who were serving life sentences for the murder of Carl Bridgewater, had only recently come down from the roof of Long Lartin after a demonstration against their convictions. The Home Office were not pleased with the consequent publicity which saw television camera crews outside the gates and quite a lot of press coverage. Their predictable response had been to fit anti-climbing devices along the top of the roof to prevent any further demonstrations.

The anti-climbing devices consisted of two pieces of metal grille, four foot long and one foot wide, slotted together to form a cross. Through the centre of the cross ran a metal bar around which the two pieces of grille revolved in an X shape. They were fitted to brackets along the guttering such that they fell out and away from the roof if any weight was placed on them. For ten days myself and the man who was to come with me on the roof, Stephen Robson from Cardiff serving a nine-year sentence for robbery, racked our brains over the problem. The date of the climb was set for Boxing Day; though we were committed to it, we weren't about to miss our Christmas turkey nor extra food which would come in handy later on, if only we could figure out a way to get on the roof. I was walking around the exercise yard on a crisp winter morning, staring at the roof, when the solution suddenly dawned, and it was not so much my ingenuity as their error that supplied it: the devices were too close to the top landing of cells.

The cell blocks in Long Lartin were three-storey buildings with a pointed apex roof. The window ledge on the top landing of cells was only three feet away from the guttering that held the anti-climbing devices and the coils of razor wire. If we could get a person to lock himself in a cell on the top floor and slide out a board from the top of the window, that would enable us to climb closer to the roof than the window ledge allowed, and would also give us enough room to step back and over the devices; like walking the plank!

Steve's brother, Alan, volunteered to barricade himself in the cell and during the next two weeks we set about getting the thing planned. We collected five locker tops, each of plywood one inch thick and six foot long, which we nailed and glued on top of each other. We scoured the wings for canvas mattress covers which we cut up and sewed into a bell tent. For cooking we took a large tin and thousands of matchsticks, using boot polish as a firelighter. Clothing was not too difficult to get hold of and food was in reasonable supply. To make our protest known we purloined a tin of white paint and a hundred party-size balloons – marketing the product was all the rage in the early 1980s. I had bought the balloons from the prison canteen, under the guise of wanting to 'spruce the wing up for Christmas'.

The climb up to the roof was not without its problems. Stephen scaled the knotted sheet and stepped over the climbing devices without any trouble, but it took me fifteen minutes of hard work to get up to the third-floor window ledge and then pass all of the stuff from the cell to the roof while sitting astride the board balanced precariously out of the third-floor window. However, within an hour of setting off at 10.30 a.m. on a crisp though not cold Boxing Day, we were encamped on the roof, tent pitched, stove burning and a delightful cup of tea in our hands to celebrate our ascent; the screws were running around like lunatics. The governor, as he told me later, was 'quite pissed off' with our protest and he had his officers in the security department, who were responsible for the anti-climbing devices, filling in paperwork for a month.

The views from the roof of Long Lartin maximum-security prison are really quite spectacular and you can see all over the Vale of Evesham. Visitors to the prison waved at us in support, while the press took photographs of the roof, now emblazoned with our slogan: 'NO PAROLE = NO CONTROL'. The negotiating officer sent by the governor visited each day and made lukewarm promises which amounted to nothing of substance. Of course we knew before we went up there that our protest would not bring about any changes to the new parole system, but that did not, in my view, make it any less valid.

The inmates were still allowed out on exercise each day and we had total support. Each morning a breakfast of eggs and bacon was passed up from the lads in the wing, though it would have to come from a different cell each day because of the spies the governor had planted to 'interdict' us. We had plenty of food, however, and the tent stood up well to the wind. On the first Saturday morning of our stay, which lasted for twelve days in all, we spent the morning blowing up the balloons, and when the visitors arrived that afternoon we let most of them go, each bearing the message of our protest, and they carried on going for miles and miles. We released the rest while the lads were on exercise the next morning – a huge roar went up as they sailed high over the razor wire and into freedom!

When we eventually came down from the roof at 8 p.m. on 7 January 1984, we were taken straight to the punishment block but, contrary to our fears, were not manhandled; instead they gave us a supper of chips, fried eggs and bacon, a hot shower and then banged us up for the night. Tired as we were, it was going to be 2 a.m. before we got to sleep. The block was full of people who'd passed food up to us and whom the governor would not allow back to the wing until we had come down. Stephen's brother, Alan, charged with 'conspiracy to help prisoners climb up on the roof', was also present and eager to hear of our news.

The punishment block at Long Lartin is totally separate from the prison wings. It is a square two-storey building with an enclosed exercise yard in the middle. There are visits each day from the doctor and the governor. The governor we called Flash-Bang because of the speed of his rounds: flashing past your just-opened door just as they banged it shut again. Toilets were fitted in the cells, but as they had been fitted by the somewhat sub-standard prison works department, there were a number of problems. The toilets were fitted back-to-back so the toilet in one cell backed on to the one next door, sharing a common wastepipe. When the person in the cell next to mine had a crap and pulled the chain, his turds would appear in my toilet bowl. The next twenty minutes would then be taken up with each of us flushing our toilets in the hope that, between us, we could get the turds back on course.

The morning after we came down, I was charged with climbing on to the roof and the case was remanded by the governor for hearing before the BOV. During the course of the following week one of the lads in the block was taken into a strip cell by staff and beaten for refusing to put his mattress outside his door. The atmosphere in a maximum-security prison is delicate at any time, and that tipped the scales. That night the dozen of us who were down there smashed the cells to pieces, ripped out water pipes and flooded the wing, broke lockers, smashed windows and tore clothing to shreds. The governor responded by sending in the now disbanded Minimum Use of Force Tactical Intervention squad (MUFTI squad).

When the BOV sat to hear our cases the following week I was facing three charges: climbing on the roof, smashing up the block and being in a television-room sit-down protest that had caught up with me from the previous November. Everyone refused to appear before the Board and the result was a rather swift finding of guilt and punishment aplenty. I was sentenced to lose 120 days remission for the rooftop protest, 119 days for smashing up the block and three days for the sit-down protest. All of these came with their usual allies of Cellular Confinement, Stoppage of Earnings and Loss of all Privileges for fifty-six days. Within half an hour of being sentenced by the BOV, I was in a taxi with three officers on my way to Dartmoor.

> HM Prison Dartmoor is a forbidding establishment in an isolated location on the outskirts of Princetown in Devon. Its isolation and grim reputation led to a decision in 1960 that it should be closed. However, a rising inmate population since then has meant that it has been kept open and there are extensive plans for rebuilding.

Not the claims of a penal reform body, but the opening words of the Home Office in evidence to the Woolf Inquiry.

Dartmoor escaped closure in 1960 and was similarly reprieved two years later. In 1974 the Prisons Board decided on its 'progressive rundown' but never got within three years of even starting it and, in 1979, Home Secretary William

Whitelaw not only overruled its closure but guaranteed that it would 'remain open indefinitely'. This was in direct defiance of the recommendation by the 1979 Committee of Inquiry into the UK Penal System, chaired by Mr Justice May, that Dartmoor should be closed because it was 'nowadays simply against nature'. According to Lord Justice Woolf, in April 1990, 'Dartmoor still fully justifies its awesome reputation.'

As the taxi pulled off the A38 northeast of Plymouth and began its long journey across Dartmoor, the disc jockey on the local radio station began to play 'The Long and Winding Road' which ever since I have associated with that journey. On our arrival at the prison, despite it being 11 p.m. there was a reception committee waiting. The long corridor down to the block was filled with prison officers and I was frog-marched to E Hall which, for the next eight weeks, was to be my home.

E Hall is a brutal place and I witnessed many prisoners being beaten there as well as suffering it myself. I was placed in a cell and strip-searched. Then they took all of my clothing and gave me a pair of filthy overalls to wear, switched off the light, closed the door and left me alone in the darkness to contemplate my future.

The cell had a small concrete platform some six inches from the floor on which was a thin mattress. There were no sheets or blankets and the piss-pot in the corner gave off a foul smell. I lay on the bed and listened to the water dripping down from the roof into the bucket placed behind the door to collect it. I felt the first cockroach climbing on me about an hour later and brushed it off with a flick of the hand. But not only were they persistent, they also had force of numbers and before the night was out I'd killed twenty-three of them – it was a way of passing the time.

The next morning I heard my name being called from a window and was delighted to find Trevor Smith just a few doors down from me. He had been with me in the block at Long Lartin and had been shipped to Dartmoor because the screws up there couldn't cope with him.

I got a letter from Pat Wilson that day. While at Long Lartin I'd started studying electronics, along with the lad across the corridor from me who was also interested in the subject. This friendship resulted in an occasional letter from his parents-in-law Pat and Arthur Wilson who, unknown to me, were supplying him with most of the answers to the maths questions! I was amazed to receive this letter from Pat, who lived in the Warmley area of Bristol, because she had only written to me a few times before and it had usually been no more than a few lines of 'hope you are well', etc. However, she had heard about my nights on the tiles and had tracked me to Dartmoor. I wrote back the same day though I had to rewrite the letter because the censor stated I had 'made allegations' which I had not previously ventilated through the complaints procedure.

I knew that I had to survive the next fifty-six days of punishment with as little trouble as possible. From what I had seen of Dartmoor from my previous stay, which was remarkably free from hassle, and from what I had now seen of E Hall, I knew it would not be easy; and I was right.

For the next fifty-six days I lay in my cell, which was devoid of all furniture during the day as the mattress and blankets each morning had to be placed outside the door – I was finally issued with blankets not because I was cold without them, but because the rules state a man on punishment has to put his blankets outside the cells, which he can't do if he doesn't have any. We were permitted one bath per week and one change of clothes. The water was brown and the clothes ill-fitting and ancient. Slop out took place after each meal. One trip to the recess was allowed and it became a matter of juggling with the water bowl, piss-pot and eating utensils while making sure that you did not cross any of the white lines the screws had painted on the floor to mark where you were allowed to walk; this was 1984, remember.

I was allowed to have my legal textbooks with me after much hassle and a promise not to allow others to read them; something I did not have the slightest intention of complying with. I doubt whether any student ever had the peace and quiet that Dartmoor afforded me and I ploughed on, thoroughly engrossed in my subject. Talking was not allowed, though we used to hold quite good conversations by using the heating pipes: placing your ear on top and shouting through a cupped hand on to the pipe was quite a good means of communication. It was not all doom and gloom, however, and this period of my life was greatly cheered up by the antics of Bill Flynn.

Six foot two inches, barely nine stone, and with an admirable fondness for baiting prison officers, Bill Flynn brought me many happy hours of laughter. He was always being dragged down the block for winding up the screws and was a great one for playing practical jokes. Though the screws abused him as they did everyone else, he managed to keep a smile on his face as well as on mine. He did, however, have one weakness; Bill loved a cigarette. Punishment meant little to him so long as he could have a smoke, and the screws of course went out of their way to make sure he didn't get it. One day while we were both visiting the punishment-wing library, a converted cell on the upper landing of the two-storey block, Bill – who hadn't had a smoke in three days – spotted that the screw sitting at the table outside the door was smoking a pipe and his eyes lit up at the prospect of a few drags.

I don't think the screw stood much of a chance once the decision had been made. Bill brought his books to the screw seated at the table and, as the screw picked up the first one, Bill was around the back of him in a flash, scooping up the pipe. He ran down the landing, puffing furiously on the purloined instrument. The screw was in shock for at least five seconds and then the shout went out, and screws appeared from the skirting boards and dashed off in pursuit. Bill, who was puffing away as if there was no tomorrow while I had tears of laughter running down my cheeks, was rapidly disappearing behind a cloud of smoke. It took them only a minute or two to catch him, but prising the pipe out of his mouth took them five times as long. He received five days extra punishment for his cheek; but he hadn't finished yet.

The following week when we visited the library the screw was waiting for us and was not going to make the same mistake again. He knew that Bill was watching him as he carefully filled his pipe, and Bill in turn was wise enough to know it was a wind-up. As we came out of the library and placed our books on the table, the screw looked at Bill and put down his pipe making sure they both knew it wasn't lit. He slowly checked off the library books and returned them to Bill, who then calmly walked around the back of him, picked up the pipe and placed it bowl first into the steaming cup of coffee by the screw's hand, smiled and walked away as if nothing had happened.

During the first two weeks I saw three prisoners beaten by officers in E Hall. I am well aware that many people believe that such brutality does not exist in our prisons, or that a 'clip around the ear never hurt anyone'. The first view takes innocence to the point of idiocy, while the second stretches innocence to the very edge of dishonesty. At the recent inquest into the death of 58-year-old Germain Alexander in Brixton prison, the postmortem on his body revealed more than eighty bruises, a fracture of his lower spine, and two of his teeth lodged in his windpipe. The inquest, which lasted for nine days, failed to discover how he had sustained these injuries while locked inside a strip cell in the hospital wing of the prison. Brutality breeds brutality and I know from my own personal experience the physical and mental damage it can cause. Until you have lain awake at night, as I have done, fantasising about how you would kill a person who had harmed and brutalised you, then you have not yet conceived the meaning of 'hatred'. You have to experience the isolation and brutality that I and many other prisoners have suffered before you can appreciate the damage caused by a prison regime. And do not easily discard from your thinking the fact that these people are one day going to be turned loose in society – and their next victim could be anything from your home to your loved one.

The day my punishment ended I expected to be moved, either back to Long Lartin or to another prison. The governor who visited me that morning said that he would speak with me later about it – I hadn't asked, and as usual I ignored his presence completely. At lunchtime I was called to see the governor who told me that as a result of my fairly good behaviour during my stay he had 'persuaded Region' that he should keep me. That was the last thing I wanted. He was not even going to allow me to go on the prison wing; he wished to keep me segregated for the Good Order and Discipline of the prison under the infamous Rule 43. I told him in no uncertain terms that he could fuck himself, there was no way I was staying at Dartmoor and if they wanted a fight about it, they could have it. I was dragged back to my cell, screaming abuse, and locked up.

I managed to speak with Trevor Smith, the cheerful 23-year-old black guy from London. He was also off punishment but still segregated for Good Order and Discipline. We both decided that the time had come for action. The following morning I formally applied to the governor for a transfer, but he was having none of it. 'I told you yesterday you are not going anywhere, so you may as well get used to it.' We'd see about that. The next morning, when I was told to move to another cell to stop me having a conversation with Trevor, I refused. They came to my door twice before they brought the MUFTI squad in to remove me to the strip cell.

I was smashed against the back wall of my cell by riot shields and my legs were cut from under me by a hefty clout from a four-foot wooden stave. I was then dragged from the cell in a body belt, a strong leather belt with metal handcuffs which pinion the hands at the side, and placed into one of the three strip cells at the end of the landing. The strip cell, built totally within another cell, triple-doored and with half-a-dozen cubes of frosted glass for a window, is a bleak and forbidding compartment. The walls had once been painted white, though now they bore only the stains of human excreta and decaying food. The bed is a small concrete platform and the cell, like all other cells in the punishment block at Dartmoor, contains a tree stump bolted to the floor for a chair.

I was sitting in the middle of the cell when I heard the outer doors opening an hour or so later. My lip was split where my tooth had come through, my right eye was closed by swelling and my wrists were locked painfully inside the body belt. When the door opened I found myself confronted by six uniformed prison officers. Two of them stepped forward and removed the body belt. A man in civilian dress standing between them looked at me, nodded just once and the door was closed three seconds later without a word having been spoken; I had just been 'examined' by a doctor from the Prison Medical Service (PMS).

There has been a statutory medical presence in our prisons since 1774, though the PMS itself was created as a separate medical body more than a century later by the Prison Act 1898. It remained separate in 1948 when the National Health Service was established and today it continues to stand isolated and alone, amid growing calls for its abolition and integration into the mainstream NHS.

There are three types of doctor employed by the PMS: full-time prison medical officers (PMOs) who are civil servants; part-time general practitioners, and visiting specialists. In May 1990 the hundred PMOs were assisted in their duties by 1,069 uniformed prison 'hospital officers', only 171 (16 per cent) of whom had even basic nursing qualifications. The Royal College of Nursing has described their 24-week training course – raised from thirteen weeks in 1983 – as 'grossly inadequate' while the Prison Officers' Association has conceded that 'it is little more than an extended first-aid course'. At the inquest into the death of Germain Alexander, one hospital officer admitted that he had no formal nursing qualifications at all, but was responsible for the 231 prisoners located in the acute psychiatric unit of the prison. The future of the PMS is unclear, but its condition is firmly on the critical list.

It was a few hours after the doctor 'examined' me that I distantly heard the tea trolley being brought round, followed by a commotion and then the shouting of voices outside the cell. I learnt a few minutes later that Trevor Smith was in the strip cell next door to me after allegedly upturning the tea trolley and assaulting two officers. When the staff had collected new rations and opened the second door in the block, they were met by Royston Gaylard who, they alleged, repeated the efforts of Trevor Smith to protest at the treatment I'd received, and they bundled him into the only remaining strip cell.

I knew I was in for another beating – and I wasn't mistaken – so I began 'shitting up'. I look back now and wonder how on earth I could have sunk to such a level, but when you are treated like an animal you invariably begin to act like one. I knew that if they came in for me I'd have to do the only thing they couldn't abide, which was to hit them with shit; ironically they had to feed me and so it was a weapon they could never remove.

When the door opened and half a dozen officers faced me it was clear that the shit put them off. I was standing against the back wall, turds in both hands and screaming abuse at them. They decided that discretion was the better part of valour and withdrew. I heard them going into the strip cells where Royston and Trevor were located and listened to the noises as they carted them away to a destination I found out later was Exeter.

They returned to me later with the suitable protection of brown overalls and riot helmets. I was crashed to the ground, had my hands cuffed behind my back and was bodily carried

90

out of the block to a transit van. I was kicked as I lay bundled on the floor, all the way to Exeter. I thought as I left that I had achieved my transfer, but it was not to be. When we arrived at Exeter the governor refused to accept me because he was already holding Trevor and Royston. Alas for me it was to be another trip down the long and winding road with a few more kicks to make sure I hadn't 'gone to sleep down there'. I arrived back at Dartmoor and was once again taken to the punishment block where I was segregated in the strip cell for the Good Order, etc.

As I write this, I have before me a copy of the official request made by the governor of Dartmoor to the prison's BOV, who were required to grant authority if the segregation was to continue beyond the first twenty-four hours – it had already been three days in my case. In support of his application to the BOV the governor had written the following:

> Just completed punishment for serious offences at Long Lartin. Has been involved in subversion in E Hall – inciting other prisoners to start a 'Dirty Protest' and to create disturbances in which staff were injured. A thoroughly offensive, dangerous and disruptive man.

Not surprisingly, the BOV granted him one month's segregation, renewable each month, but I was destined to remain there for only half that period. The senior medical officer at Dartmoor was, at that time, Dr D'Arcy-Smith, a man who had a drink problem and who I suspected learnt his medicine in the concentration camps. He is dead now, and I have no regrets, for he was responsible for so much of what was wrong at Dartmoor. He came to 'examine' me a few times while I was in the strip cell, but it was always done from a distance of six feet.

To be locked in a strip cell can be horrific, particularly after the first day or so. It is almost deathly quiet and with artificial light you lose all track of time. There is nothing to occupy you except the thought of the next beating or jug of cold water that might come your way. Paranoia sets in and every minute is as long as a leap year. Totally isolated and at the complete mercy of the authorities, it is a formidable weapon they hold, made all the more powerful because the use of strip cells is not subject to any procedural safeguards. When those three doors slam shut, all the applications for judicial review and all the courts of human rights in the world are light years away.

When the 1964 Prison Rules were being debated, Lord Elwyn Jones, then MP for West Ham, and later Lord Chancellor, said that solitary confinement was 'about the cruellest form of punishment, short of actual physical torture, which one human being could impose on another'. As I look back on the effect it had on me, I can only say that it reduced me to an animal of the lowest instincts.

As the first week passed and I was still confined to the strip cell, I realised that if I was ever to get out of Dartmoor only desperate measures would achieve it; I knew what had to be done and I began to plan it as best I could. The governor visited each morning but rarely spoke and we just looked at each other with hatred over the mammoth penal divide that separated our lives. One day the following week, as I distantly heard the slamming of doors, I stood ready for his visit. When the outer doors opened and we confronted each other, I asked him if I could speak with him for a few moments. Quite taken aback by my politeness he stepped past the screw in the doorway and came into the cell; he never even saw it coming. Behind my back I held a turd which I rammed into his face as soon as he approached. He was choking and the screws pounced as I screamed abuse at him, my fingers pushing the shit up his nose and into his mouth. That is the stark reality of the damage solitary confinement does and yet, even as I write, for thousands of men and women in prisons up and down the country, a brutal strip cell is still a daily reality.

Within an hour I was bundled on to the floor of a yellow transit van, tied up in a body belt, and taken up the M5 to

Bristol, where the governor made it clear he didn't want me and where I made it clear that the feeling was mutual. The block at Bristol is only a small one, no more than half a dozen cells the size of broom cupboards. The governor, I must admit, did try to be helpful and even put me on the landing at one point. I lasted less than an hour before throwing a cup of tea over the landing screw.

The only good thing about my time at Bristol came as a result of the correspondence I had kept up with Pat Wilson. As she lived in Bristol she arranged to come and visit me. On the day of the visit I went over to the visiting room to be met by a lady I would guess was in her late forties. She had driven the eight miles from her home on her motor bike and arrived in her oilskins. We soon discovered it was a small world: she and her husband Arthur – whom I was to meet a week or so later – not only came from Manchester, but Pat came from the same district as I did.

From Bristol prison I was put 'on the Ghostrain' as it is known to prisoners – 'on circuit' as it is known to the authorities. This involves being carted from one end of the country to the other, often late at night or early in the morning, and always without notice. You are not allowed to settle into any kind of regime; transfer can come at any time. I've been moved from a prison after as little as twenty-four hours though normally it occurred every ten to fourteen days. They do not tell you when you are going or where, and they are not above a little bit of deception. Being called for a visit, wanted by probation and even required to see the chaplain are just a few of the many excuses they've used before kidnapping me and dragging me into the back of a van.

Once you are on the Ghostrain everything goes haywire. Your property never travels with you, nor does your money, which is always sent on later. Except of course it never quite catches up with you; by the time your money arrives at a prison, you've probably been gone a week. My property has been sent to prisons I've never been to and a great deal of it was lost entirely – which gave rise to my numerous actions against the Home Office for negligence.

During the following few months I visited a total of thirteen prisons before I found myself down the block at Swansea. I had by this time been working hard on my legal studies and the block at Swansea was not too bad, comparatively speaking. The two block officers, Chislett and Carlson, were not out to fight the world or make a name for themselves, they just wanted a quiet life. The governor was approaching retirement and didn't want his block turned into a battleground. All in all, I was left in peace to study. It was at Swansea that I scored my first try against the Home Office Prison Department, in the Swansea County Court, for negligent loss of property – winning £134 plus costs, and interest at 15 per cent!

By February 1985, after more than a year being shunted around the penal system on the Ghostrain, I found myself on a car ferry bound for my second taste of the dispersal system at Parkhurst prison on the Isle of Wight. By this time I had accumulated over 200 disciplinary reports and had lost in excess of 500 days remission. Like all other such dispersal prisons, Parkhurst was maximum security, though it also contained a special security block (SSB) which had been the initial lamentable response of the Home Office to the escapes of Wilson and Biggs. The SSB at Parkhurst was opened in August 1966; two months later George Blake escaped from Wormwood Scrubs and the consequence was the Mountbatten Report which paved the way to the dispersal system and security classification.

My time in Parkhurst, on the whole, was relatively good; the prison was run on fairly liberal lines and most prisoners spent their day high on dope or drunk on hooch, and I was no exception. I had grown used to cannabis while on the Ghostrain and soon became mentally hooked on a spliff for bed. I also tried, though just once, snorting speed. I remember being persuaded to have a line and then waiting for what I

94

assumed would be a high, but little seemed to happen. As 10 p.m. approached I decided to get into bed. Out of the corner of my eye I saw a matchstick on the floor; and that was the start of it. I spent the whole night cleaning the cell. I made the bed a dozen times, scrubbed the floor until it shone and was whistling and singing away until my next door neighbour banged on the wall at 5.30 a.m. and told me to 'shut the fuck up'. Never again!

I used to smoke cannabis through a clear 'BiC' pen using a technique, common in prison, called 'spotting'. I would break down the dope into very small pieces, put the lit end of a cigarette on a spot and pick it up. As it began to burn I would inhale the smoke through the pen case – having taken out the refill of course! But this practice was soon to land me in trouble and it took a trip all the way to the House of Lords to get out of it.

On 13 March 1985 I was idling my time in the fabrication shop when I was pulled out by two security screws (known as Burglars) who took me back to my cell for a special search. Cell searches in maximum-security prisons are an accepted, though resented, way of life. When we were in the cell one of the officers, Malcolm 'Taff' Long, immediately spotted an unlawful second mattress and informed me that I was on report. The second man, Officer May, looked through my pen holder – which contained about thirty pens – and pulled out the one I had used for spotting only that morning. I was relieved to see that I'd remembered to put the refill back. After smelling the inside of the pen, he informed me that I was on report 'for having in your possession a biro pen case adapted for the smoking of a controlled drug' – who, me?

The following morning I was taken down to the punishment block where I was charged with the two offences. As soon as I saw the charge from Officer Long I knew I'd have little problem getting the case of the extra mattress dismissed; in his efforts to convict me, he'd charged me under the wrong paragraph. Instead of charging me with possession of an unauthorised mattress, he went for a breach of good order and discipline; a mistake which cost him the game. The pen, however, was another matter. I knew that if the pen was sent away for forensic examination that would give me four weeks to come up with some kind of defence. When the case came before the governor later that morning, I formally pleaded not guilty and requested that the pen be sent away for forensic analysis. The governor agreed and I was allowed back up on to the wing. I then had to suss out where I was going to take it from there. However, news of the 'no case to answer' in the matter of the extra mattress soon became common knowledge and added to the reputation that I was rapidly building of 'being a bit of a bloody Rumpole'.

I spent a few weeks searching through legal textbooks and reading case law before I first spotted what I thought was the best bet. It depended on the reporting officer not knowing the law of evidence, and of that there was a reasonable chance. The pen had been sent away for forensic examination to London, where it would be examined and returned to the prison with a statement from the person responsible for conducting the tests. What I counted on was that neither the governor nor the reporting officer would be aware that the forensic report, as evidence by itself, was not worth the paper it was written on; without the author being present and available for cross-examination, it was hearsay and thus not admissible. When the pen came back, 'having proved positive for cannabis', I was taken back down the block. The governor was away on leave and his place was taken by his deputy, Governor Trufett.

With everyone assembled in the room the governor asked whether I had received a copy of the forensic report, which I agreed I had. I again pleaded not guilty and the governor read out the forensic report and promptly found me guilty. I explained that in his haste he had not allowed me to cross-examine the reporting officer, whereupon I was permitted to ask a few questions. The reporting officer admitted that the pen, by itself, was not an unauthorised article, 'but it has become an unauthorised article because in this case it has come into contact with a controlled drug,' he opined, or, as the governor put it, 'it's authorised for writing bloody letters, Leech, not for smoking dope'.

As the case for the prosecution closed with no sign of the forensic officer, I made a submission of 'no case to answer' and explained to the governor that as a pen was not an unauthorised article the charge must be dismissed because there was no admissible evidence to show that it had been used for anything other than the purpose for which it was authorised. All of this sailed completely over the head of the governor, who told me that he was not going to allow me to 'drag this adjudication on, or call witnesses'. He again found me guilty and ordered that I lose twenty-eight days remission; had Rumpole come unstuck?

I returned to my cell and looked up the case law on prison governors' disciplinary adjudications, with the intention of applying to the High Court for judicial review; the news was not good. The case of *St Germain*, in 1978, had held that the disciplinary adjudications of prisons' BOVs were directly reviewable in the courts but, because of what lawyers call obiter dicta, prison governors' adjudications did not have to be treated in the same way. The Court of Appeal in a totally illogical and perverse judgement, had held in the case of *King v. Deputy Governor of Camphill Prison* ([1984] 3 All ER 897), that a prison governor's disciplinary adjudication was not susceptible to direct challenge in the High Court by way of judicial review; despite discharging precisely the same functions under a common disciplinary code as the BOV.

The three appeal court judges in the case of *King* stated that a governor was only a 'manager' of a prison, responsible to the Secretary of State. 'If a prisoner is dissatisfied with a prison governor's adjudication', said Lord Justice Lawton, 'he can petition the Secretary of State and invite him to correct the error of the governor.' If the Secretary of State refused, ran the reasoning, then the prisoner could review the refusal of the Home Secretary in the courts; but he could not review the governor. Two of the three judges who reached this conclusion, expressly admitted in their judgements that their conclusion was 'illogical'.

Being faced then with no alternative but to petition the Home Secretary, I did precisely that, the same day that Governor Trufett passed his sentence. I also took up the matter with Lord Avebury, a liberal peer in the House of Lords who was interested in matters penal. On my behalf he wrote to the Home Office. While I was waiting for the Home Office reply to come back, I made contact with a solicitor who has probably done more to develop prisoners' rights and to remedy injustices than anyone else I know, Kate Akester of solicitors B.M. Birnberg & Co., London SE1. I came to know Kate very well. She has a deep-rooted sense of justice and is a mine of information on the penal system. Kate had represented Nicholas King in the Camphill case and I learnt that the search was on to find a case to take to the House of Lords to overturn the Court of Appeal's decision that governors were not reviewable.

Stephen Sedley QC, another champion of prisoners' rights, was also eager to get a case to the Lords, but the Home Office had a decision in *King* which they liked a great deal and were not about to give up without a fight. Because the Court of Appeal is bound by its own previous decisions, the only court that could overturn *King* was the House of Lords. But, as the Home Office was well aware, the Lords will not listen to 'academic' cases nor pronounce on abstract questions of law – judicial review is available to correct a present situation, not a past one.

Once a prisoner had appealed a disciplinary adjudication, by way of petition, and had that petition refused, he was then eligible to make the long journey to the Lords. But the Home Office was extremely vigilant. In every case where a prisoner –

after refusal of the petition – had sought leave to apply for judicial review, the Home Office suffered an immediate change of heart, quashed the adjudication, returned the remission and effectively prevented the whole issue of whether governors were reviewable from reaching the Lords by rendering the case academic.

On 25 June 1985, I received a letter from Lord Avebury, enclosing one from Lord Glenarthur, the then Home Office Minister in the Lords responsible for prisons. This is what he said:

> I have carefully studied the transcript of the adjudication at which Mr Leech was found guilty of having in his possession a biro pen case adapted for the smoking of a controlled drug. As Mr Leech said, the adjudicating Governor found him guilty immediately after reading out the forensic report and before Mr Leech was given any opportunity to make his defence or cross-examine the Reporting Officer. Although Mr Leech was then allowed to ask some questions it seems clear that his defence has been prejudiced. I therefore consider the finding of guilt unsafe and have decided to exercise the Secretary of State's power under Prison Rule 56(1) to remit the punishment made against Mr Leech.

During my time at Parkhurst I had a total of five cases against the Home Office in the Newport County Court, whose profits were all ploughed back into the 'business' to help fund the next action. One day I was called to see the governor who informed me he was stopping a letter I had that day sent to my solicitor, on the grounds that it contained allegations against the prison authorities which had not yet been ventilated through the internal complaints procedure – the Simultaneous Ventilation Rule again. However, this time the governor was not only wide of the mark, he was also standing on the very edge of a contempt of court; the SVR had been quashed by the High Court twelve months previously – so far as letters to solicitors were concerned – in the case of *Anderson v. Secretary of State* (1984). I argued with him for ten minutes, but he would not hear of it. Turning to his chief officer as I left I heard him say, 'I feel a summons coming on, Chief.' He was right, and I served it on him personally at 10 a.m. two days later. Ultimately, in that case, the Home Office corrected the error of the governor and the letter went on its way, just as I did a week later – making, in June 1985, my second trip to Maidstone prison.

At Maidstone prison I found that the Rev. Peter Timms had left the prison service to take up a full-time ministry, but the legacy of his progressive reign could still be felt. While at Maidstone on this occasion I met again an old friend I had earlier known at Wormwood Scrubs, Colin Davies, who was serving life for murder. I first met Colin through his interest in music. He was a typical Welshman, with crotchets and semibreves flowing through his veins, and he could almost make the piano sit up and talk. During the six months I knew him, he taught me how to read music, though I was not the best of pupils, and we spent many hours discussing the inhumanity of the life sentence he was serving.

Three years into his life sentence, in June 1977, the Home Secretary informed Colin that his case for release on licence would next be reviewed in June 1984 – known as seven-year knock-back. Throughout 1985, as he waited each day for his answer to arrive, Colin spoke to me about his plans for his release. He wanted to go to college to study for a degree in music and intended to live back in his native South Wales. Each day I lived with his hopes and his fears and each day we both waited for the answer to arrive from P2 Division at the Home Office. Normally an answer takes a year to arrive and as we entered July I watched Colin each day become more and more convinced that this time the news would be good. 'If they were going to knock me back, Mark,' he told me one day, 'they would have told me long before now.'

I watched him sit in his cell day after day, behind a door that was slightly ajar, watching the notice board on which the names of those required by the governor were posted each lunchtime. His world revolved around getting his answer. One day I returned late to the wing at lunchtime to find that Colin's name was on the board for call-up and I dashed to his cell to hear what even I believed was good news. I had been in his cell numerous times but I knew as I opened the door this time that the news was not good.

Colin sat on his bed, his dinner untouched on the table, his head in his hands and his body heaving as he tried to choke back the sobs between the words that came out in short bursts. 'Why, Mark . . . I can't understand it . . . why me . . . why now?' I had nothing to say to him at all. I saw the 'answer' lying on the table and picked it up. 'The Secretary of State has fully and sympathetically considered your case for release, but has regretfully concluded not to authorise it on this occasion.' It went on to say that Colin's case for release would next be considered in June 1992; Colin Davies had just received his second seven-year knock-back.

I put my arm around the man who was probably the kindest and gentlest man I had ever known, and as he cried out his pain I could feel only hatred for the inhumane life-sentence system which caused such heartache and anguish. There were no explanations for why he had not been given a release date, nothing to soften the blow or help him be more prepared to present his case next time. He had his hopes built up and torn down, reassembled only to be destroyed; and his family, too, had to travel this emotional roller coaster. I last saw Colin Davies a week later. He was playing the piano in the church and as always made the music sound so graceful. Afterwards he brought me a book of his poems and we had a cup of tea in my cell. I will leave the final verdict on the life-sentence system to Colin, who wrote this seven days after he received his second seven-year knock-back, and a week before he tragically put his words into action in his cell at Maidstone prison:

Death must be a fairer place
than this infernal strife,
'tis better dead and buried
than locked away for life.
'Tis better warm beneath the soil
than waking up alone,
to find yourself alive in hell
enclosed in steel and stone.
Waking to the sound of keys
opening up your tomb,
doors that crash like cymbals
inside a concave room.
Yes, Death must be a fairer place
than this infernal strife,
'tis better dead and buried
than locked away for life.

One day, shortly after Colin's death, I formally applied to the prison governor for a copy of my disciplinary adjudications, and I was amazed to find that it still contained the conviction for the pen case which, from the letter of Lord Glenarthur, I thought had been quashed. The search was still on for a case with which to challenge in the House of Lords the illogical conclusions of the Court of Appeal in *King*. As I lay in my cell I read again the letter from Lord Glenarthur; he was quite clear that he considered 'the finding of guilt unsafe' and yet the conviction still stood. It wasn't until I read again the wording of Rule 56(1) to which he referred that I spotted what everyone else seemed to have missed: the Home Secretary did not have the power to quash a conviction, only 'remit or mitigate' a sentence – the days of the *King* judgement were numbered.

I realised that I would have to tread carefully on this, so as not to alert the Home Office until it was too late. I formally petitioned the Home Secretary again on 8 October 1985 and this time I specifically asked him to quash the conviction which was still recorded on my record and which Lord Glenarthur himself admitted was 'unsafe'. On 23 December 1985, the Home Secretary replied that he had no power under Rule 56(1) to quash a conviction – a three-year journey to the House of Lords was underway. The Court of Appeal in *King*, in their haste to close the court-room doors to direct judicial review of governors' disciplinary adjudications, had failed even to look at whether the Home Secretary had the powers to dispense the remedy that they said he could. I learnt from the Appeal Court in *King* that before coming to the courts I first had to travel down the Home Office avenue and invite the Secretary of State to put right the governor's wrong; but, in reality, it wasn't an avenue so much as a cul-de-sac.

Edward Fitzgerald is a barrister in the same mould as Stephen Sedley QC. He, along with Kate and Stephen, had acted for Nick King in the Court of Appeal, and I rang him at his chambers one afternoon with the news of what I had discovered. He was delighted, and we set about making an application for judicial review to quash the conviction still recorded against me. The Home Office were now in a quandary. They could not render my case academic because they had already restored the twenty-eight days remission, and they could not quash the conviction I was seeking to quash because they had no powers in law to do so. But they were still not about to give up without a fight. I had never been surprised before by anything the Home Office got up to, but on this occasion I was absolutely astounded to discover the lengths to which they were prepared to go to defeat the case.

Maidstone does not like litigious prisoners and when I issued a summons in Maidstone County Court over the loss of my property, which I discovered was missing from the reception, I was abruptly transferred to Lewes prison in Sussex. I lasted three days on the wing before I first visited the punishment block. The following three weeks saw me making more visits to the same place, each on a disciplinary report and each finding being case dismissed. The staff were not at all pleased about it and the governor finally segregated me for Good Order and Discipline in the punishment block where I made the profitable acquaintance of Prison Officer Stanley Turner.

Officer Turner has been in the prison service many years and, while other inmates may have got along with him, I could not abide his attitude and his ideas of how a prison officer should behave. One evening in my cell in the block I rang my cell bell to discover that he was the only officer on duty. I heard him come out of the office and cancel the tally which falls on the Cell Call Register Board. Without even bothering to look in my cell, where I had fallen and hurt my head and my back, he went back to the office shouting, 'I'll be with you in an hour.' He was as good as his word and returned an hour later with the senior officer. When I asked him why he had not answered my bell, he replied that I was 'always fucking ringing it'. As a plea of mitigation for his failure to do his duty, that had the persuasiveness of a Party Political Broadcast.

The prison doctor came and examined me, and left some painkillers. The following morning I put down to see the governor and complained about Officer Turner and his lack of attention to duty. The governor told me to make a written complaint and I handed this in for investigation. A week later I was called to see the governor who informed me that Officer Turner had admitted failing to answer my cell bell. He apologised and said the matter would not happen again – I felt a summons coming on! A week later I served a County Court summons on the Home Office asserting negligence against the Prison Department, and their servant Officer Turner, demanding £110 in damages and costs for his failure to answer my cell bell; having admitted it in writing to the governor there was very little they could say. Two hours after I received the Home Office cheque for £110 a month later, I was once again kidnapped and thrown into the back of a taxi bound for Wandsworth; no sense of humour these prison officers.

On arrival at Wanno, as it's known throughout the penal system, I was placed straight down the block for the Good Order and Discipline of the prison. I soon discovered that it deserved every inch of its awesome reputation for violence and brutality. Within an hour of being placed in the block at Wandsworth, news of the success against the Home Office in the Cell Bell case was transmitted along the officers' grapevine. I was in the cell when three officers came in and started to push me around: 'How about suing us then, bastard?' I was more than willing to do as they asked, and simply bided my time for the moment.

While at Wandsworth Kate came to see me and we began getting the case together against the deputy governor of Parkhurst. Because of the precedent in the case of *King* we knew that the only way of winning was to get to the House of Lords. But it is a feature of our legal system that no matter how high up the legal pipeline the blockage may be, you still have to start from the bottom. In the interim few months we had been working hard on the case and had discovered a recent and highly illuminating judgement of the Northern Ireland Court of Appeal in *McKiernan v. Governor of the Maze Prison* ([1985] 6 NIJB). The Northern Ireland Court of Appeal, which had been referred to the judgement of their English counterparts in the case of *King*, refused to follow it and held that for prisoners in Northern Ireland, prison governors' disciplinary adjudications were directly reviewable in the High Court. This created the situation where there was a difference of opinion between the Court of Appeal in Northern Ireland, which held that prisoners could review the disciplinary adjudications of governors, and the decision of the English Court of Appeal, which held that they could not.

When we lodged our application for judicial review against

the deputy governor of Parkhurst, the matter first came before Mr Justice Mann as it is necessary in such proceedings to obtain the leave (permission) of a High Court judge. Mr Justice Mann was of course referred to the *McKiernan* case but held, quite correctly, that he was bound not by the Court of Appeal and *McKiernan* in Belfast, but the Court of Appeal and *King* in London. He refused our application, as he was obliged to do, and we began preparing for the next battle with the Court of Appeal.

While down the block at Wandsworth, I was thrust back into a regime every bit as brutal as that at Dartmoor. I was assaulted twice by prison officers and spent five days in the strip cell. I was never placed on report in connection with these incidents but I did twice try to persuade the magistrates at the local court to issue summonses against named officers for assault. The elderly lady on the bench, when I appeared handcuffed to two prison officers, refused each time I asked, rolling the words 'assaulted by prison officers' down her nose in such a way as to leave me in no doubt that she thought I was telling lies; I later discovered she was a member of the BOV at Pentonville.

In July 1986 I was moved first to Norwich prison and then to Blundeston, a closed, category B, training prison on the outskirts of Lowestoft. I was first employed in the printing shop which turned out huge amounts of literature and stationery for the prison service. I lasted only a few weeks before I was carted down the block 'on suspicion of breaking into the canteen'. I shit up twice while I was down there and became more and more subversive, spending time in the strip cell and body belt as a result. Release was only nine months away at this time and Pat Wilson, who had kept in touch with me throughout my sentence, had offered me a home with her and her husband on release. Down the block I completed another three cases against the Home Office in the County Court at Lowestoft and was working hard on the case against the deputy governor of Parkhurst which was heard in the

Court of Appeal on 10 September 1986 – by a man later to become well known to prisoners, Lord Justice Woolf.

When I heard the case was to go before Woolf, I feared the worst. Before becoming a judge in the early 1980s, Harry Woolf had been the in-house counsel for the Home Office Prison Department, the Patriot missile used to defend them against attack. He had been very successful, and that did not give me a great deal of hope. However, Harry Woolf as a judge has earned a reputation for fairness and professionalism the envy of his peers. When the case came before him he listened carefully to the arguments before granting leave to move for judicial review, but refusing the application to quash the conviction; like Mr Justice Mann in the High Court, he too was bound by the previous decision in *King*. Lord Justice Woolf refused leave to appeal to the House of Lords, deciding that 'their Lordships themselves should be the ones who decide whether this case is the appropriate vehicle with which to challenge the decision of this court in *King*'.

While I was locked in the block at Blundeston, Kate, Edward, and Stephen Sedley QC were working hard compiling an application for leave to appeal to the House of Lords; in the end the document ran to over fifty pages and was lodged at the judicial office on 2 October 1986. It was to be heard by the House of Lords a month later on 6 November, and the Home Office was just about to play its last card in the hope of rendering the case academic.

On 19 October I was abruptly released from the block and given a place on G Wing. The following morning I was seen by an assistant governor who inquired whether I wished to attend the hearing of the application for leave to appeal in the House of Lords on 6 November. I refused to discuss the case with him and gave him the name and telephone number of Kate Akester. At 3 p.m. I was once again called to see the assistant governor, this time accompanied by two screws, and I thought that yet again I was being ghosted; I was right, but it was a different type of train they were putting me on. As I entered his office I knew something was different when he asked me to sit down. I refused and said that I preferred to stand. He then held up a piece of paper and told me that he'd 'just had this through from the Home Office'. He would not show me the paper or its contents, but he informed me that the net result was that I was free to go; I was poleaxed.

The Home Office had done the only thing it was able to do to defeat this case. They could not render the case academic by restoring my remission, because they had already done that and I was complaining about the conviction. They could not quash the conviction because they had no power to do so. The only thing left was to give me back heaps of lost remission to ensure that my release date came before the hearing on 6 November. At 5 p.m. on 20 October 1986, after almost five years in prison – and four months before I was due to be released – I was dumped at Lowestoft train station with traffic whizzing past me and people rushing here, there and everywhere. It was mind-blowing. They had given me a travel warrant for the train to Bristol, but there were no trains running because of an industrial dispute. I did have my driving licence and so I hired a car and drove the 300 miles to Bristol.

When the Home Office, in their efforts to render the case academic, gave me back remission that I had lost, they miscalculated by a week. I should have been released not on October 20, but on October 13. I claimed from the Home Office damages for that week and was rewarded with £280.

I had telephoned Pat Wilson before I left Blundeston prison and also called Kate at home to inform her of developments; she was as poleaxed as I had been. Driving 300 miles when you haven't been behind the wheel of a car for five years comes as a shock. It took me over seven hours to drive to Bristol where I met Pat's husband, Arthur, in a layby just off junction 18 of the M4 at about half past midnight.

The next few days were a hive of activity. I could not sit still for a minute, wanting to cram everything in and afraid to go to sleep in case I missed something. I saw a friend who ran a printing business and for £50 he produced an excellent set of naval discharge papers which purported to confirm that I had just served twelve years in the Royal Navy as a lieutenant, instead of five years in prison as a 'thoroughly offensive, dangerous and disruptive man'. Within a few days, and with the help of these documents, I obtained employment as the area security manager for a company based in Bristol called McQueens. The name on the documents was Mark Sinclair-Smith and that is the name I thereafter masqueraded under.

McQueens supplied security guards to various department stores, warehouses and industrial estates and my job was to travel around the locations in my area and confirm that things were running smoothly. One of the companies McQueens had a contract with was the major international superstore group, Toys 'Я' Us, based in Reading. There were two stores in my area, Bristol and Woking, and I regularly visited each one. A few weeks after I joined McQueens I was approached by Toys 'Я' Us and invited to apply for the vacant position of Head of Security (UK). My initial reaction was to decline the invitation because I was already happy with my job at McQueens and a bird in the hand is worth two in the bush. I had the secure job with McQueens, while the naval discharge papers might not stand the scrutiny which Toys 'Я' Us would, I thought, have put them through.

A week or so after the initial approach I was again invited to apply and in the end I did so, having my first interview with the then Director of Personnel, Roger Phillips, in his office at Reading. The following week, on Monday, 8 December 1986, I again attended the offices of Toys 'Я' Us and was interviewed by both the Managing Director, David Rurka, and Roger Phillips. At the end of the interview, which went well, they told me that as far as they were concerned I could have the job, but they first wanted me to have a chat with their Corporate Head of Security, Wayne McBrian. I agreed, and was then told Mr McBrian resided in the USA. They flew me to New York the following Friday, and accommodated me in the Ramada Inn at Rochelle Park, New Jersey, for the weekend. The interview on the Sunday morning went well, and I had been back in the UK a day when David Rurka phoned to tell me that I was the new Head of Security for Toys 'Я' Us in the United Kingdom. I had keys to every store, possessed all the alarm codes and safe combinations, was on a salary with bonuses of £22,000 a year and was given a company car; I had been out of prison for precisely eight weeks.

My new job carried a great deal of pressure. I could have walked into any store in the UK and emptied the safe at any time, but I didn't. The figures we are talking about are far from insignificant, but I genuinely wanted to leave crime behind me; despite the fact that I'd got the job fraudulently in the first place. One of the greatest hurdles a discharged prisoner faces when he leaves prison is getting a job. The first question any employer will ask is where you have been working for the last few years; being honest at that point carries with it the likelihood that you will remain unemployed. From the very first day, therefore, the discharged prisoner has to start rebuilding his life on a foundation of lies in order to survive; the debt to society may have been paid, but the receipts are never destroyed.

I thought I knew all about pressure and had experienced hard times, but working for TRU – as it was known – I soon discovered that an 18-hour day was not at all unusual. I was often away at 6.30 a.m. and would spend the day travelling around the stores conducting security audits. I would arrive back at the Head Office about 8 p.m. and spend two hours completing necessary paperwork before driving the 115 miles back home to Bristol where I would fall into bed exhausted; often to be woken during the night to be informed about intruder alarms that had gone off in various stores. Despite the tremendous pressure I was under, I enjoyed the job and it was a stepping stone to bigger and better things. One afternoon I received a telephone call from a director of a well-known multinational company inviting me to apply for the position of non-executive director of security (UK) – I declined. I decided to stick with what I already had. But my time at Toys 'Я' Us was about to come to an abrupt end.

The Director of Personnel, Roger Phillips, asked me one day for a copy of my birth certificate for pension purposes, but I did not possess a birth certificate in the name of Sinclair-Smith and I kept putting him off. In the end he became suspicious and gave me an ultimatum: produce the certificate by Monday, 9 February 1987, or leave the company. To leave would not have meant the matter was laid to rest. Suspicions would have been aroused, police called in and arrest but a short step away. I spent the weekend before February 9 in Norwich with some friends, leaving at about 7.30 p.m. for the trip back to Bristol. As I was approaching Reading on the M4 I pulled off for petrol at the Penta garage on the Basingstoke Road, where TRU had an account. I then went the 250 yards to the office and collected some papers. The next day I knew would bring the police unless I could produce the birth certificate and as I sat there in my office I realised that it was over. Quite why I went downstairs and destroyed the records store and computer room by setting fire to them, later said by the police to have been akin to taking a sledgehammer to crack a nut, I don't know, but that is what I did.

I then continued down the M4 towards Bristol, but had not gone more than ten miles when my bleeper went off and informed me there was a fire at the Reading Head Office; it did not come as a surprise. Not to have responded would have been to invite attention, so I swung the car around and headed back up the M4 to Reading, where I found the place swarming with police officers and firemen. I am an atheist when it comes to matters religious, but as I swung the car into the car park I recall saying to myself, 'God, if you just get me out of this mess, I won't do anything ever again'; I'm still an atheist!

I finally got to bed at midday the following day and fell into a deep sleep. I was woken by Pat Wilson at 2.30 p.m. to say that there was a Detective Sergeant King on the phone from Reading and he insisted on talking to me. To say that he invited me to Reading Police Station would be an understatement; it was a case of come or be brought. I made an appointment for 6 p.m. that evening and was packing for Europe within three minutes of putting down the phone, the thought of sleep obliterated. I spent the next month in Europe travelling from Amsterdam to Barcelona via Belgium, West Germany, Switzerland and France; all courtesy of a certain 'Listening Bank', which spent too much time listening and not enough time looking.

The pressure of the last few months had a great effect on my mental state and I feel sure that had I been examined on my return to the UK in March 1987, I would not have been allowed out on the streets. To have described me as 'paranoid' would have been to describe the sun as 'warm'. When I phoned Pat and Arthur on my return, they were pleased to hear from me, but a little distant and I got the impression – wrongly it transpires – that they didn't really want anything to do with me. I stayed with them for a few weeks, but my attitude was causing them strain which they did not deserve. One evening they told me that if the police came for me, they would tell them I was there. I 'knew', as only someone who is paranoid can know, that they were on one side and I was on the other. I left the house taking with me a cheque book and Barclaycard – and I shall regret it to my grave.

In my car I had the uniform of a naval lieutenant and I took to wearing it as a disguise – at least in my fuddled brain that was the reason. I was walking in and out of military bases masquerading as an officer. In North Wales I stole a number of two-way radios and went up to Scotland to sell them. In the car park at Glencoe I lay back in the sunshine and rolled a joint, soon becoming high and forgetting all about my problems, which were piling up around me. One of the radios was on and tuned into the Mountain Rescue frequency, and I could hear that there was a rescue going on in the hills. I decided in my confused state to join in and picked up the handset saying I was stuck on the mountain; I thought at the time it was a laugh, but it was only a few years later that I really understood the wicked thing I had done.

When I was arrested in Edinburgh Castle two days later, still wearing the uniform of the naval lieutenant, I was surprised that they had sussed out that I wasn't quite 'kosher'; only later did I learn that Edinburgh Castle is the home base of the Royal Military Police for the whole of Scotland! When I was arrested by a sergeant in the Special Investigations Branch of the military police, he was a little unsure as to whether I was who I said I was, a naval lieutenant. During the walk to the guard room two military police corporals walked past us and the sergeant gave them a dressing down for 'not saluting this officer'. They became worried as the hours went by and I would not tell them anything; I was ultimately arrested under the Prevention of Terrorism Act because they thought I was involved in such things; to which I readily confessed. For the next three days the bomb disposal people blew up four sites around Scotland where I told them I had hidden weapons.

I was charged with a whole list of offences and placed on remand at Porterfield prison in Inverness. Many of the staff at the prison had relatives involved with mountain rescue work and I became a target for their hostility. On 30 June 1987 I was assaulted by three officers in the association room of the prison; four years later that case is still winding its way through the courts. Letters to my solicitors were either not sent or read first by the staff, and I started legal action over this in the Court of Session. Inverness is a small prison with a big reputation, where they have the infamous Inverness Cages for recalcitrant prisoners, and brutality is the rule not the exception.

When I subsequently appeared before Lord MacDonald and his jury at the Inverness High Court on 2 August 1987, I pleaded not guilty to all charges. Pat and Arthur came up from Bristol for the trial and appeared as witnesses for the crown because of the cheque book. It was as I was sitting there in the dock feeling all pompous and important that I suddenly felt, for the second time in my life, the real feelings of guilt. I looked across at Pat as she stood in the witness box and my heart went out to her and Arthur. These people who had done more for me than almost anyone else stood in the witness box a few feet away and the tears came to my eyes; I needed help. I was subsequently sentenced to six years for all offences and sent back to Inverness and a few days later arrived at Perth prison where I was to spend the next ten months.

While I was there, on 4 February 1988, almost three years after the disciplinary adjudication that started it, the House of Lords handed down a unanimous decision in *Leech v Deputy Governor of Parkhurst Prison* ([1988] 1 All ER, 485 (HL)) which overturned the decision in *King*, and held that the disciplinary adjudications of prison governors were, like those of a BOV, directly reviewable in the courts.

Sergeant King and Detective Constable Phil Allen in Reading, meanwhile, had not given up hope of getting their hands on me and succeeded in having me extradited from Scotland to face the arson charges in Reading Crown Court. I arrived in Reading prison on 5 April 1988 and found myself next door to the cell in which Oscar Wilde had been incarcerated almost a century before. When he wrote his famous *Ballad of Reading Gaol* he did so under the pseudonym of 'C.3.3' which many people have since wrongly claimed was his prison number; in fact, it was his cell location.

I had a very good solicitor acting for me, Lynne Griffiths of Griffiths Robertson, and she was a great help, sorting out the defence in a manner for which I can have only the highest praise. It was clear that I needed psychiatric help. The long years of solitary confinement and the pressure and mental damage that brings with it meant that the only way I was ever going to get out of this vicious imprisonment cycle was with the medical help which everyone knew I needed. While I was waiting for the appearance at Reading Crown Court, my sister

Yvonne came back into my life after almost ten years absence. She had been divorced by her husband Kevin for her adultery with an ex-policeman and since then had picked up the threads of her life and achieved great success. She left school without any qualifications at all, but following her divorce she attended night classes and passed her O and A levels before going at the age of forty-two to Salford University and taking a Bachelor of Science degree with Honours; and she wasn't finished yet. She then went to Harvard University in the States and completed a Master's degree in education, before returning to live and work in Oxford.

But Yvonne and I have never really got on and probably never will. I have the greatest respect – pride would not be an inappropriate word – for what she has achieved in the last ten years, but we can never seem to see eye to eye; she still looks upon me as the small eight-year-old. She made her reappearance in my life while I was on remand at Reading and, within a few weeks, seemed to almost take over not only the running of my life, but my defence as well; but Yvonne's like that. I knew she had only my best interests at heart, but I resented this intrusion. My family have never really done anything for me with the exception of my dad and I have little time for them now. Yvonne came to my trial at Reading Crown Court, as did Pat and Arthur, who had decided that I was worth a second chance and have stood by me throughout all the trials and tribulations I have since been through. His Honour Judge Rose had before him two psychiatric reports from doctors who had interviewed me and recommended a place at Grendon Underwood – Britain's only therapeutic prison. I was sentenced to three years imprisonment for the Toys 'R' Us arson, to run concurrently with the six years I was already serving, and I went first to Reading prison and then to Winchester, to await what I was told would be a place at Grendon 'just after Christmas' 1988. The officers in the allocation unit clearly had difficulty spelling 'Grendon', because the prison named on the allocation form I received was 'Dartmoor'.

I tried every way I knew to get out of the allocation to Dartmoor; I knew it would be a retrograde step for me. The screws at Dartmoor have long memories and they would not have forgotten the mini-riot in the punishment block in 1984. I wrote to my MP who took the matter up with the Home Office and I also wrote directly to the governor of Dartmoor asking for his help to get the allocation changed. Lynne Griffiths also wrote and Pat took to writing weekly postcards to the Home Office to convince them that this was not in my best interests. In the final analysis it was all wasted. The Home Office and the allocation unit at Winchester were not in the least bit interested in such trivial things as individual prisoners; I was a prisoner and I would go where I was told. I left Winchester for Dartmoor on 12 January 1989, with a sense of foreboding which knotted my stomach. This was the very last thing I needed.

My arrival at Dartmoor proved that nothing had changed. They remembered me only too well and placed me on the landing which was overseen by the same two officers who had been injured in the disturbance five years previously. For the next two weeks my life was made a misery. I was left locked up all day, my door was kicked at periodic intervals during the night and I was 'missed' for meals on a number of occasions. I was assaulted twice by the staff and my efforts to issue proceedings in the Plymouth Magistrates' Court came to nothing because the prison governor John May — whom Lord Justice Woolf felt to be a governor of the 'highest calibre' — refused to give me the full names of the officers so that the summonses could be issued. The only thing that kept me together at this point was the thought that I would soon be going to Grendon. I had already made great improvements in the last few months and I knew that if I could just get to Grendon I could pour all of this shit out of me and start to get on with living a normal, crime-free life.

By 27 January 1989 I had taken just about as much as I

could take without reacting in the only way I knew how. I applied to see the senior medical officer and was called to see him one afternoon. I told him what was happening and how desperately I needed to get out of Dartmoor for Grendon. He pulled out my medical record and told me that there was no mention of me going to Grendon. 'They only take people in their last six months', he told me incorrectly, 'so you're not going anywhere for at least another two and a half years.' I was devastated. I could take no more. I returned to the wing and was locked up. When the time came for slop out at 6 p.m., I grabbed the first person to walk past the door – a prisoner called Samuels – and dragged him into the cell. There is no doubt that I was out of control and for the next six hours I kept him in the cell, tied hand and foot while I ranted and raved about what they were doing to me. In the end I cooled down and came out to be taken to the punishment block while the authorities at Dartmoor set about covering their arses; as the riot eighteen months later revealed, the time was fast approaching when the prisoners at Dartmoor would take no more.

I was charged by the police and got the services of a brilliant solicitor in Exeter, Chris Over of Crosse & Crosse. When I eventually appeared at the court in April 1989, Chris gave the magistrates the whole background to the event. We fully expected the case to be committed to the Plymouth Crown Court for sentence, but they were lenient beyond almost my wildest expectations: I received a consecutive sentence of four months imprisonment.

I was in the block at Dartmoor for six months after the hostage incident and there were still no plans to move me to Grendon until at least the following year; the reason they brought it forward could not have been more tragic.

I am no stranger to prison suicides, having seen more than a dozen of my friends over the years choose death in preference to continued imprisonment, and the death of David Greenhow on 8 May 1989 was every bit as devastating as those that went before. David Greenhow, serving a three-year sentence for burglary, was just twenty-three when they found him hanging from his cell bars in the punishment block of Dartmoor prison.

Immature, with learning problems, David had been a difficult prisoner in the eyes of the prison authorities. After banging on his cell door one lunchtime and annoying prison officers, the governor ordered that he be taken to the punishment block and segregated for the Good Order and Discipline of the prison. When David arrived in the block on Friday, 5 May 1989, he was immediately placed in the strip cell, the favoured response of the prison authorities to any prisoner who will not, for whatever reason, do as he is told. He was not charged with any disciplinary offence and had not been violent; he didn't know why he had been banging his cell door. I have no need to imagine how he felt at being locked in that strip cell, for I have spent many long and lonely nights in precisely the same place. It is not the place to confine an animal, much less a confused and disturbed young man.

The prison's BOV did not visit David while he was confined for the weekend in the strip cell; instead they gave their authority for the segregation to continue by a telephone call to the prison. The handbook of the Association of members of the Boards of Visitors (AmBOV) states that 'a well-intentioned authority' can only come from visiting the prison, 'it cannot be done over the telephone'. David was released from the strip cell on Monday, 8 May, and placed into the punishment cell next door to my own. During the afternoon exercise period he asked to return to his cell and, as he left the yard, I was left with the impression of a young man more in need of help than punishment.

It was just two hours later, during the evening slop out, that they discovered him hanging by a bed sheet from his cell bars. Resuscitation equipment took fifteen minutes to arrive from the prison hospital, by which time, despite strenuous efforts to revive him, David was beyond all help and a crushing atmosphere of failure descended on all in the vicinity.

Throughout the evening the various authorities associated with death arrived, including the BOV who obviously felt this merited a visit to the prison in person. At 11 p.m. I lay in the darkened silence of my prison cell, with tears of sadness and frustration once again on my cheeks, and listened to the echoing noises as prison staff removed his body from the cell next door. As David was being taken through the prison gates for the final time, a prison official would somewhere have been completing the bureaucratic paperwork, a process which includes stamping the front of his prison record with 'Discharged: Dead'.

To those familiar with the workings of the penal system, the fact that David Greenhow was not identified as a suicide risk, despite having made a number of previous attempts, will not come as any surprise; official reports reveal it is a frequent failure. In 1990 Dr Edna Dooley, consultant forensic psychiatrist at Broadmoor hospital, published in the *British Journal of Psychiatry* (1990, 156, 40) the results of her study of prison suicides in England and Wales between 1972 and 1987. During this period, in which 300 prisoners took their own lives, Dr Dooley reported that the increase in prison suicides was 'far greater than might have been predicted from the rise in the prison population'.

Dr Dooley reported that 126 of these prisoners (43 per cent of cases) had a record of previous suicide attempts. A quarter had received some form of psychotropic medication in the month prior to their death and sixty-five (22 per cent) had not only made a previous suicide attempt, but had done so at least once during their current sentence. There was a record of psychiatric treatment in a quarter of all cases, eighty (27 per cent) had previously been psychiatric in-patients and more than half had a record of alcohol problems or drug abuse.

The death of people like David Greenhow tragically illustrates that conditions within our penal system are such that a young man, with decades of his life stretching out before him, chose to sacrifice the whole of his future rather than face just one more day in prison – and in doing so, he made a statement about our penal system far more damning than a dozen Woolf Reports could ever be.

Following the death of David Greenhow, I wrote to the police and the local coroner at Tavistock, asking that I be allowed to attend the inquest to give evidence of the circumstances and conditions which David experienced during his final few days of life. Despite writing three further letters I never had a reply from either of them, and I suspect the letters never left the prison. I wrote a letter about David's death to the *Guardian* which, when published on 13 May 1989, resulted in more than a hundred letters from decent people as far away as Switzerland. The prison authorities, however, were not going to allow me within fifty miles of the inquest. My cell door was opened at 6 a.m. on Thursday, 11 May and I was told that I was moving to HM Prison Grendon Underwood – right there and then.

PART THREE

Therapeutically Speaking

The Regime at HM Prison Grendon Underwood

In 1939 the famous Prison Commissioner Sir Norwood East and the director of the Prison Medical Service, Dr W Hubert, presented their report to the Home Secretary on 'The Psychological Treatment of Crime', in which they recommended the establishment of a 'psychiatric prison'.

Twenty-three years later, in September 1962, that recommendation was put into practice with the opening of HM Prison Grendon Underwood. Some twelve miles from the town of Aylesbury in the quiet Buckinghamshire countryside, Grendon sits behind the open prison of Springhill and both prisons share the same governor. In 1970 the director of the PMS, Dr Pickering, wrote: 'Grendon is not a hospital but an integral part of the Prison Service; it does not take patients eligible to be dealt with under the Mental Health Act; it is therefore complementary, rather than supplementary, to the Special Hospitals and psychiatric hospitals of the NHS.'

The regime at Grendon Underwood is based on the group-therapy system first developed at the Henderson Hospital in Surrey, which is why there is closeness between Grendon and the Henderson to this day. In its thirty-year history, Grendon's therapeutic penal regime has not been duplicated elsewhere within the UK, though lukewarm promises continue to be made. In the government's white paper, *Custody, Care and*

Justice, published on 16 September 1991 in response to the Woolf Report, Home Secretary Kenneth Baker promised that his efforts to create more 'active regimes' in prison would include extending the experience learned at Grendon Underwood; but similar political promises in the past have not been transformed into penal practice. Michael Selby, the then governor of Grendon (he retired at the end of 1991, after thirty-seven years in the prison service) is the first in its history not to be medically qualified; a point seized upon by those who believe the objective is not to extend the Grendon regime, but to reduce it.

Throughout this chapter I have altered the names of all inmates to protect their identity.

I arrived at Grendon Underwood at 5 p.m. on Thursday, 11 May 1989. The atmosphere was totally different from the one I had left behind me that morning in the mists of sodden Dartmoor. Here there were pleasant gardens blooming with flowers and people with smiles on their faces. The reception, a small single-storey building close to the gate lodge, was also noticeably different. The reception procedure was over very quickly and the screws 'asked' you to wait in the waiting room, rather than barking the usual order.

All new arrivals at Grendon – and all prisoners who come are volunteers – are accepted only on the basis that they satisfactorily complete a two-month assessment on the A Wing Assessment Unit (AU). The AU is situated two-thirds of the way down the long M1 corridor which connects all the various therapeutic wings together. As I picked up my kit from the reception and began to walk down the long sloping M1 corridor, I wondered what the next few months held for me. I had just come out of six months segregation in Dartmoor and my attitude was what it had always been: subversive. Though I really wanted to change my way of life, I knew that the battle to achieve that change was not going to be easy. I had heard many things about Grendon and not all of them were complimentary.

I stopped outside the AU main door, my kit in one hand and my belongings in the other, and I felt as I stepped over the threshold that all of my fears had been justified; it was going to be the hardest battle of my life. Once inside the wing, I was asked to wait while the screw went off to answer a distantly ringing telephone. As I stood there and looked around me I wondered whether I really knew what I was doing. My feelings were running high. I had not been left alone outside of a cell for almost the whole of the last year. As I looked around me, standing just inside the door of the AU, I saw a dining hall to my left, which I later discovered doubled as a games room, and opposite this the wing office.

I found out later that the wing office was rarely used by staff. They much preferred to use the censors' office down the passage as it contained a kettle, cooker and fridge, and became a sort of unofficial staff room. The wing was silent as I stood there; the forty or so inmates who were then on the wing were locked in their cells between 5 and 6 p.m. while the staff went for their tea. The walls were covered with bright posters advertising games competitions and the wing rules. The pastel-coloured walls were clean and there was a marked absence of the graffiti which is part of the fabric of any penal establishment. The floors were highly polished and the whole building actually smelt clean and fresh.

When the screw came back from answering the telephone, he opened the wing office and invited me to come in and sit down. He wrote something in a book and then asked me my name. When I replied 'CF1449 Leech', he wrote that down and then asked, 'And what do people call you?' Well, that had me stumped. I could think of any number of answers to fit that particular question, but I simply repeated my name and number. At that point he asked me where I had come from and when I told him Dartmoor he nodded and said, 'I thought so. We do things differently here, as you'll see.' He looked through my prison record and said, 'Right, Mark, what's your religion and diet?' I was still trying to suss out the angle with the first name so I answered automatically, 'Vegetarian and Mormon.' He never seemed to question it, simply wrote down what I had told him. 'My name,' he said, 'is Rob George. I'm one of the officers attached to the AU staff. I'll organise a meal for you now and then we'll get you upstairs and you can sort out your cell.'

The rest of the evening went by in a blur. I was seen by the wing chairman, who I was absolutely astonished to find was a prisoner and who told me the regime and routine of the AU. The wing principal officer wanted to see me next, but I managed to swerve him until the following day. I was then taken into the censors' office and issued with six letters and six visiting orders, despite the fact that I was bang up to date with both.

The AU did not mix with the rest of the prison and had its own exercise time. Inmates on the AU were not a part of the Grendon process until they were accepted into therapy at the end of their two-months assessment. There was very little work to do on the AU in the physical sense, with the exception of the wing cleaners and the two pantry men who dished out the meals and did the washing up. I was told that the job of pantry man was the only job in the AU which was issued by the staff and it carried with it a number of perks in addition to extra food. The two pantry men did not get banged up during the dinner and tea-time lock-up periods and were the highest paid on the wing. As a consequence, I thought, only the screws' favourites would be bestowed with that particular job; they were people who needed to be 'watched' without a doubt!

Therapy as practised in the rest of the establishment did not take place in the AU. There were no group meetings (mainly because there were no 'groups'), though the wing as a whole did meet three times a week. The inmates elected their own chairman and vice-chairman, in which staff had no right to vote – I warmed to the place a little after hearing of their exclusion – and each of the tri-weekly wing meetings were used for inmates approaching the end of their stay in the AU to give their life story.

This is a harrowing experience. You need to take the plunge and reveal things which you have probably never spoken about in your life before and you have to tell them to forty people you have known for only a matter of weeks. Can you imagine telling your life story, including all those little skeletons hanging in the closet which you would not normally disclose either through embarrassment or because of the pain they bring? Yet that is what has to be done, for a major part of the Grendon regime depends on breaking the dishonest habits of a lifetime. The two months I spent on the AU were the most difficult I had ever spent in prison, up to that point at least, and telling my life story was something I dreaded from the very beginning.

There are new arrivals into Grendon each week and the staff hold their own weekly meetings to discuss the fate of those who arrived eight weeks before and had therefore reached the stage where a decision on their future had to be made. The voting system for staff is the same as that for inmates: each person has one vote and a simple majority carries the day. I now had eight weeks in front of me and no idea of what lay ahead. The first shock to the system was not long in arriving.

The morning after I arrived I was called to see the wing principal officer whom I had successfully avoided the night before. The hour that I spent with Ian Booth only added to the confusion already raging within me. I faced a man in his mid-forties, neatly dressed in uniform with two pips on each shoulder displaying his rank. He asked me about my past and I noticed that throughout our conversation he did not take notes; prison officers *always* take notes, either as a result of an inability to recall basic facts or the system's need for raw data. He asked me about Dartmoor and the solitary confinement I had come from. His office was nicely furnished and I clearly recall the warning notice on his wall: 'A lack of planning on your part does not constitute an emergency on mine.' As we sat and talked lightly about things in general, I gradually began to relax, for Ian Booth possesses an ability to make people feel at ease. Ours, however, was not so much a conversation as a monologue from him; it was impossible for me to forget that he was dressed in the cloak of authority.

I returned to my cell and pushed the door to. The cell locks in Grendon are sprung each morning to prevent you from banging yourself away, since the regime is based on self-confrontation, not seeking solitude and hiding your anxieties behind a cell door. I lay there and went over and over the deep-seated confusion raging inside me. I had a hatred for prison officers and knew that those of a senior rank had only achieved their office by condoning brutality and being more of a bastard than their colleagues. The abuses within our penal system take hold because those higher up the ladder refuse to do anything about them; I was not impressed by pips. But somehow this Ian Booth seemed different. He had not wanted to know anything that anyone else would not have felt free to ask, and he didn't probe or patronise. He was an enigma, to be watched with care and marked down as 'slippery'. I knew, as only someone who has been through the system can know, that there is no such being as a good screw.

The following morning I met the wing tutor, Annette Tyler, who had been at Grendon for longer than anyone could seem to remember. Plump, middle-aged and forthright, she represented my mother and I took an instant dislike to her; a dislike I later realised was wrongly placed. Annette was a member of the wing staff on the AU and she was responsible for conducting the almost daily group in social, life and communication skills. My initial meeting with her was as brief as I could make it and our relationship was destined to be stormy; she too had been marked down as 'slippery'.

At 10.15 a.m. on the day after my arrival, the large wing bell was rung by the chairman signifying time for the tri-weekly meeting. Forty or so chairs were spread out around the large, oblong, television room. The wing chairman, Dave, brought the meeting to order, while the vice-chairman sat next to him and wrote down the minutes of the meeting. I was totally dumbfounded by it all. You have to be a part of the prison system to realise just how outlandish all of this was. Here was a group of forty prisoners sitting in a room with three officers and a female; and they were all chatting away as if they were the best of friends discussing where they were going for a drink that night. The system was being turned on its head.

Because there was a new member of the wing present – me – all the people in the room, including staff, had to introduce themselves by name, starting with the chairman. It was then that I realised the very dangerous people Grendon held. Inmates introduced themselves by their name, offence and sentence. 'My name's Joe Bloggs, serving eight years for drugs', or 'My name's John Smith, serving ten years for rape and buggery'. It was a bold introduction and left people in no doubt that Grendon looked not to the crime – as the system does – but to the criminal. When my turn came I managed to get out my name and details before collapsing back into my chair, grateful that attention had now been focused on the next man.

The meeting began with the chairman asking for 'minutes'. I expected this to consist of reading out the minutes of the last meeting, but discovered that it takes its name from the people who had collared the chairman before the meeting to ask for a minute to bring something up they felt was important and should be discussed. As I sat there I heard the first man who'd asked for a minute verbally castigate for his attitude a screw he called 'Steve'. The air was thick with verbal abuse and I fully expected it to 'go off' – to get out of hand – but it didn't. The screw didn't deny what had been said about his attitude, but he made clear that he, unlike us, had never asked to come to Grendon in the first place. The next minute came from a lad who complained that the prisoner next door to him was playing his radio too loud at night. He said that he had asked him on a number of occasions to turn it down after 10 p.m. but the lad had not taken any notice; I was shell-shocked. Here we had a prisoner openly grassing up another prisoner in front of not only the wing staff, but the whole complement of inmates as well. Inside I was screaming, '*you fucking scumbag!*' To make it worse, the lad who complained was a sex offender while the person complained about was serving twelve years for robbery. The rebuke, however, was taken, much to my surprise, and the wing was told that the radio would be turned down after 10 p.m. I could not take all this in, it was against every bit of 'nick culture' that I had ever known; and there was more to come.

Paul, who was serving a five-year sentence for rape, was due to give his life story – or 'wing talk' as it was known. This experience would ultimately come to each of us, but for me at that time it was impossible to sit there and listen to him making his excuses. He had been talking for fifteen minutes when I decided that I had had quite enough of this 'therapy' and got up from my seat and walked out of the meeting; the room fell silent. I lay on my bed, my emotions washing over me, internally screaming, '*I fucking hate you!*' The guy they were all sitting there listening to was a nonce, a sex offender who had gone out and raped an eighteen-year-old girl. I hated this system which slipped nonces in by the back door and treated them better than anyone else; in reality they were nothing but scum.

I had promised Pat and Arthur that I would stay the course at Grendon, no matter what it took, but it is very easy to stand at a distance and look at Everest while passing an opinion on how easy it would be to climb. I had very quickly reached the base camp of my stay, but becoming acclimatised to the rarified atmosphere was proving difficult indeed. I seriously began to wonder, within just forty-eight hours of my arrival, how I was going to get through the next eight weeks – the thought of six months or more did not enter my head; I would not be staying that long.

I almost missed the slight knock on the door as Ian Booth pushed it open. He was a fervent non-smoker, but he held in his hand a cigarette he had obviously got from the others and which I refused with a shake of my head. I was not going to give in. What I needed was to leave Grendon as soon as possible in such a way as to save face with Pat and Arthur and blame it on the system. 'You're finding it difficult here, aren't you?' he said, moving to the cell window. Why he deliberately turned his back to me I don't know, but he was asking for trouble. 'I've just read your record, Mark, quite a chequered history you've got.' He continued to look out of the cell window at the lads playing five-a-side on the yard below. 'I know you'll find it hard here, but you can make it you know, others have done so.' I remained totally dumb, determined not to say anything to prolong the monologue. I was on the verge of telling him to get the fuck out of my cell when he turned from the window. 'Look, you have to face facts,' he said. 'You can either go on fooling everyone but yourself, or you can jump off the criminal train you've climbed aboard and start to live a better kind of life.' He walked to the door and turned as he went through it. 'The change will not be easy; like the heroin addict, there are criminal withdrawal symptoms too. The choice is yours.' As I lay on my bed listening to him walking down the stairs, my brain was in turmoil.

I do not know how long I lay there after he had gone. I felt better when I was alone; I could think straight and I knew where I stood. I was not going to be fooled a second time by authority's extended hand of kindness, which in reality contained pain and heartache. They had fucked me once; it would never happen again. I could change my life by myself. I didn't need these pseudo-psychologists to tell me where I was going wrong. I did want to change my life, I did want to leave the criminal train, but I was already on the edge of admitting defeat. I owed Pat and Arthur many things, but most of all I owed them to at least try to make both sense and success of this bewildering regime I had been thrust into. It was the prospect of telling them that I was leaving that I couldn't face; though it did not stop me wanting to get out of there as soon as I could. Another bombshell was waiting for me just around the corner.

I went down for my evening meal and was standing in the queue when I heard my name being called by a screw; I ignored him and continued to wait in the line. Screws, however, are trained to be persistent and he soon located me and took me to the wing office. Bob Young was a senior officer who had been at Grendon only a short period himself. Despite his huge size he was one of those screws who would not go out of his way in any nick to give people hassle. He had obviously been talking to Ian Booth and he asked me whether I really wanted to change my way of life. 'Come on, make a start and be bloody honest for once.' I sat there and looked at him, and slowly nodded my head. 'Yes, I want to change my life, but I don't need the nutters which this place contains to enable me to do it.' He smiled. 'When I first came here I too found it fucking difficult to come to terms with. All my service has been spent in the system and this place turns that on its head.' Huh, he could say that again! He continued, 'But after a while, when you start to see the good that this place can do – and yes it takes hard work – then you begin to realise that this is what the penal system should really be about, not banging prisoners up in strip cells and kicking all kinds of shit out of them.' I respected his honesty.

I didn't know whether I was on my arse or my elbow, so I could understand how he'd felt when he arrived. His next bit of news, however, took me completely by surprise. 'The staff have had a meeting this afternoon. One of the pantry men is leaving to go on to one of the therapy wings and we need a replacement; you've got the job.' I went to tell him that I didn't want the job, but his raised hand stopped the words in my throat. 'Don't tell me you don't want to do it. We already know that and it's part of the reason you're getting it. If you just give it a try you'll settle down and go on to better things. If you want to change your way of life, then you have to be prepared to put as much into winning that battle as you put into winning a court case and there are many staff in here who are waiting to see you fail.' There was very little I could say. I feared stepping into this unknown and alien environment, but I needed a job and so with reservations I took it, though not at all convinced that I was doing the right thing. I knew that I had to make a real decision about my life. It was easy to say, 'I want to change', but difficult to transform that wish into reality.

Drugs, sex and violence are strictly not on at Grendon, but I had indulged in all three during the large proportion of my life that I had spent in prison. From the block at Dartmoor I had brought with me a small amount of dope which I kept safely 'bottled' up my backside. I was due to start on the pantry the next morning and as I lay in my bed that night I was totally unable to sleep, despite the spliff in my hand. My brain was lit up like a pin-ball machine at Las Vegas and I struggled to work out what their motive was in giving me the job on the pantry. Prison officers always have a motive; they never do anything without an ulterior reason for doing so and I tried hard to work out what their angle was. As the darkness of the night was gently nudged out of the sky by the sunrise, I dozed off to sleep, still unable to work out what they were up to.

I very soon realised that people in this world do not give you comparatively high wages for nothing. During the course of the next few weeks I found myself responsible for counting diets, collecting meals, running backwards and forwards to the kitchen whenever we were short and doing mountains of washing-up after each meal was served. There was a dining room to clean, a floor to be polished and there was no chance of a lie-in in the morning; it was all go. Dave, my fellow pantry man, was serving a five-year sentence for grievous bodily harm and we got along quite well. He was a young lad, early twenties, and a wizard on the guitar. He had been at Grendon for almost two months and was facing his wing talk the following week. I could see that he was getting nervous about it, but I never asked him for the details of his offence; that was his business not mine.

The AU was a difficult staging post in therapy. Over an eight-week period you were shown that there are different ways of doing things other than through violence and dishonesty. I found that the AU was effectively two quite separate worlds. The world that existed up on the three landings was entirely different from the world that existed in the wing meetings. Upstairs there was not a great deal of difference between Grendon and any other prison landing. Drugs were sold, scores were settled and everyone refused to have anything to do with the sex offenders. Their cells were wrecked, piss and shit were poured into their beds by other 'decent' criminals and all in all they had a rough ride. Prisoners collected themselves into cliques, mixing with those they could trust or knew from other prisons and disregarding those they did not. I teamed up with a few guys, one of whom I shall call Alf. He was serving eight years for drugs and we got along quite well. He had been through the system as I had been and we passed our time playing chess, smoking dope and laughing at the Grendon regime; a real recipe for failure. The AU was the halfway house between the 'normal' nick and the Grendon regime and the two were frequently incompatible; and sometimes explosively so.

I had been in the AU just ten days when I was called for my first tests. For three hours I completed a maths and an English test which I was surprised to find were pitched at quite a high standard. One of the misconceptions about Grendon is that it takes people who are unable to think things through for themselves, but the reality is that only those who possess a certain level of intelligence are accepted into the therapeutic regime. During the course of the following weeks I underwent a number of other tests which appeared baffling in direct proportion to their psychological content. There were tests in 'mechanical reasoning' where you examined mechanical diagrams to determine which way the weight would go when a certain pulley was pulled. I remain baffled by many of the tests I was put through and, as a result, I find psychology a blurred form of science in which only those with degrees in the subject have any chance of understanding what the hell it is all about. I certainly understood little of it, though I 'passed' all of the various examinations I had to sit. In all I completed twenty-two hours of testing during my time in the AU and it did nothing other than lead me to suspect that the people who dream up these tests must be on drugs themselves.

I smoked the last of my dope the night before Dave, my fellow pantry man, was due to give his life story. I could see that by now he was very nervous and I sat next to him in the room as his turn came to speak about his life and what had brought him to this strange and alien place called Grendon. Dave was married with a three-year-old son and both he and his wife were heroin addicts, either injecting it (mainlining) or freebasing it on a piece of foil and inhaling the smoke, also known by the quaint name of tooting. Dave had come from a good family background and had never been in trouble other than for drugs. His family had ditched him as soon as he failed to match up to their expectations and he had fended for himself since the age of fourteen. One evening he and his wife were desperate for a fix but they had no money to buy any. His wife, a lovely girl I met on a visit one day, went out 'to earn some' and Dave was left alone in the house clucking (suffering from withdrawal symptoms) with his son upstairs in bed. The baby had teething problems and began to cry. Dave went upstairs and began to comfort the child, but no amount of rocking would stop the infant's screams. As the crying persisted, Dave became more and more unable to cope; his nerves – already raw from lack of the drug – were at breaking point.

In a fit of madness, he threw his son against the wall and he landed unconscious on the carpet. As he recounted this in a room which was totally silent, he burst into a flood of tears and my heart went out to him. He left me in no doubt that he was extremely remorseful for what he had done and it had taken a great deal of courage to talk about it. The baby survived and was currently living with foster parents while his wife successfully sought help for her addiction and gave Dave support in his own battle to defeat it. They both loved their son, of that there was no doubt. Dave's cell was full of pictures of the happy, smiling child and he knew that if they ever stood any chance of being reunited as a family unit, then the drugs had to go. He had decided to apply for a place at Grendon because he realised 'when it came down to it, that I didn't have the balls to do it by myself'.

That afternoon I was called for my first life-skills group. Annette Tyler who took the class was very good at what she did, but I could not seem to get over the barrier that lay between us. Each time I looked at her or heard her speak, I was immediately reminded of my mother, and that placed a damper on our relationship for some time. There were eight of us in the room and we all were seated in a circle. The group was going to discover the meaning of the word 'empathy' she told us, and promptly gave each of us a pencil and piece of paper. On the paper we each had to write something which for us as individuals was a very great problem, something we found hard to discuss or difficult to come to terms with. There were to be no identifying marks on the paper as each was to be anonymous. I wrote 'the problems associated with being sexually abused', folded it in two and placed it in the container she held in her hand. When everyone had done the same we then had to select from the container a piece of paper, returning it if you picked out the one you had submitted. I picked one which said, 'I do not know what love is'. It was to say the least a difficult one to select, but once you had a few moments to think about it you realised that a person who had reached adulthood without finding out what 'love' was has charted a long and lonely road.

We each then had to discuss this problem as if it was our own and, through that, we came to understand that what may at first have appeared trivial to some was in fact a living hell for others. What is it like to reach the age of thirty, say, and not know what love is? What does it say of the person's childhood and upbringing that they have never been hugged either as a child or an adult? This person, I later discovered, had lived in a home where 'sex' was a dirty word and where he had never been shown affection, and his life, as a result, was an emotional mess. He would not let people get close to him, shied away from meeting others and ended up ramming a beer glass in the face of a friend who put a hand on his shoulder to attract his attention. The person who selected my paper did very well with it considering that he had never been abused. At the end of the session I came out of the room with a very different outlook from the one I'd had when I entered two and a half hours previously; I had made my first tentative steps on the road to reform.

At this time I had still not come out and I pretended, more by omission than expression, that I was heterosexual. Coming out is a very difficult thing to do, particularly in prison, but for me it had to be done, otherwise I was simply going to go down the same road again. Why should I be ashamed of what I am? I can't change it, for the simple reason that I never created it in the first place. Those who say I can change my sexual inclination have to accept that if I can do it, so can they; I can no more become 'straight' than others can become 'bent' – we are all stuck with it. Of course people argue that homosexuality is not 'normal', but to me it is normal because it is the way I am. Those who base their arguments of normality on the fact that only a heterosexual relationship can produce children, miss a simple point: I was not born into this world with any preconceived obligation to recreate the human race.

I was in the pantry one day when Dave came in. The wing was locked up after lunch and it was my turn to wash the pots – which meant he had the back-breaking job of pushing the trolley back up the M1 to the kitchen. We began to chat about things in general while he wiped down the surfaces and I was up to my elbows in greasy water. When he asked me if I was married, I was faced with a difficult situation. Either I could say no and leave it at that, or I could explain that as the law currently stood in this archaic and bigoted country, I wasn't eligible; I took the plunge and did the latter. We discussed it for most of the afternoon and his reaction to my coming out was, 'Well, so what?' Yes indeed! Within a few days it was common knowledge in the wing and I never received any of the hassle or snide remarks that I expected to have to deal with. One afternoon a few days later I was called to see Ian Booth, who had heard the 'news'. We began to discuss the subject of being homosexual and the problems it had caused me over the years.

Slowly, but ever so slowly, my perception of prison officers was beginning to change. I found Ian an interesting person to talk to, mainly because he didn't bullshit. He knew what went on in the system and didn't either hide it or condone it. As I was leaving his office he casually asked me whether I had ever been to bed with a woman – to which I flippantly replied, with a smile on my face, 'I'm not a bloody lesbian you know!' After that our relationship went from bad to better and I began to relax for the first time in years. I had discarded one millstone which had been hanging around my neck for years and now I could stand up and say who I was without the worry of how to handle the repercussions I used to expect from it. I had climbed one hurdle in my path to therapy, but there were many more that still lay ahead of me.

I had settled in a little better than I had expected, but I was still very confused about my determination to remain at Grendon for very long. The promise I had made to Pat and Arthur, as well as to my father, was the only thing that kept me going throughout this period. Had it not been for them I would not have remained at Grendon for much longer than three or four days. But they had all stood by me when I had given them more than enough reason to walk away and for that they have my eternal thanks and gratitude. My sister, Yvonne, was still on the fringes of my life during this period. She gave me all kinds of written advice and sought permission from the authorities to become involved in the Grendon process, which was refused. Our relationship was changing and I was not easy about it. I was quite happy to have her as my sister, but not at all keen that she viewed me as her patient. I wrote to her and expressed these views and have not heard from her since.

After a month I attended my first feedback group with Annette Tyler, under the heading of communication skills. There were eight of us seated in the room, chairs placed in a circle with one chair – the hot seat – in the middle. The purpose was to discover what other people thought of you, how they saw you, and the reactions they had to your way of doing things; it was quite a startling session. Each person in turn had to sit in the hot seat and was given a number of pieces of paper on which were written such things as 'I don't trust you' or 'I like you'. The person in the middle had to give the relevant piece of paper to the person they thought most deserving of its caption. It was a heavy session.

Most of the people in the group gave me a card with the inscription, 'I find your attitude superior'. That came as one hell of a shock and it certainly gave me a great deal to think about – or 'take on board' as they say in Grendonspeak. It transpired that many people felt that I spoke down to them and further that I wanted to be in control all the time. That these statements were truthful took many months to sink in fully, but I knew from that point onward that I had a problem relating to people around me and that I had to work hard to solve it; it was not something that could be altered overnight. These feedback sessions could be very heated, but also very helpful. We all have views on how others perceive us, and they are often very different to the way in which others actually do; feedback was a way of bringing the two together. More importantly, it was a way of bringing home to each of us our own respective problems while assisting others to recognise theirs.

Body language was a subject that also came into communication skills. You learnt to recognise from people's actions when they were being defensive and when they were uptight. We 'say' far more with our bodies than we do with our mouths and learning that language gave me an advantage much later in my own therapy when I was able to gauge the effect I was having on others, allowing me to either press on or pull back.

As the date for my wing talk approached I found myself dreading it. I had by this time listened to a good many such talks and while I was moved by some, I was equally unimpressed by others which, to my mind, were nothing other than bullshit; it was interesting to note later in the year just how many of the people fell by the wayside because their commitment to therapy was not strong enough. On the morning of my wing talk I sat in the television room and tried to relax as the chairman invited the men who had asked for minutes to say their piece. When my turn came to speak I had difficulty getting the words out but the further I got into it the more relaxed I became. I fought back the tears that welled as I discussed the abuse. I had been advised not to go into it in any great depth because that was not the purpose of the life story. It found its focus in demonstrating a willingness to discuss such things, but the AU did not possess the necessary therapeutic backup which a heavy session can require. In short, it was the chance to demonstrate that you are able to discuss with others the difficult things that have happened in your life; a fundamental prerequisite for group therapy. When I had completed my life story the wing was totally silent. People just sat there and took in what I had to say and many of them came up later and said how happy they were that I had felt able to talk about things that were obviously very painful.

That night I lay in my bed and went over the events of the day in my mind. I knew that my case was due to be discussed by the staff group the following Monday and that I would hear later in the day whether I had been accepted for the Grendon therapeutic regime or would have to return to the block at Dartmoor. I wrote to Pat that night and told her how things had gone, but I didn't know at the time that she had phoned the prison to find out for herself earlier in the day; out of sight does not necessarily mean out of mind!

The following Monday I stood around anxiously along with the seven others who were that day being considered for a place at Grendon. One after another we were called into the room to be given the verdict. The criterion for a place at Grendon is that the person has demonstrated during the two-month assessment a willingness to change their criminal behaviour and has further shown that they are able to face up to their problems, which the various group sessions have revealed, and talk about them. For some, speaking in a group is just too hard, and for those there is the option of Grendon G Wing or return to prison of origin. G Wing at that time was a unit used mainly for sexual offenders and did not incorporate the group therapy that was the fundamental basis of the Grendon regime. G Wing inmates instead took part in a one-to-one therapy session, where they discussed their problems with a member of the staff or a psychiatrist. The G Wing was in the process of changing to group therapy while I was there but no permanent decision had been made as to when the regime change would take place. One of the number who waited outside the office on that Monday afternoon in late July 1989 was John. He was a recluse who took very little part in the AU regime during the eight weeks he had been there. It came as little surprise, therefore, to learn that he had been found unsuitable for group therapy but was offered a place on G Wing.

For three others that choice was not offered and they were returned to their prison of origin as being unsuitable for anything that Grendon had to offer. When my turn came to enter the room, my heart was racing. I had made a little progress since being on the AU and my relationship with staff had improved to the point where I could at least tolerate them. I had learnt that there was very little advantage to be gained from verbally abusing them for what were really the faults of the system itself, and that it was better to try to thrash out problems in a rational way. We were all in the prison system together; none of us made the rules but all of us were equally impotent to alter them. Ian Booth was seated in the room with other members of staff when I was called in and invited me to sit down opposite him. As soon as I sat down he said, 'I'll put you out of your misery – you've been accepted for Grendon group therapy.' In a strange kind of way I would have been relieved if they had rejected me, because that would have resulted in a return to Dartmoor where I could have blamed everyone and anyone for the failure to be accepted other than myself. The road ahead looked long and hard, and though I had not even stepped on to the race track, I had at least gained entry to the stadium.

On the following Monday morning I was informed that I would be moving to B Wing that afternoon. At 10 a.m. the B Wing chairman came over to see me, just to introduce himself. Peter was serving seven years for rape and had been at Grendon for two years, and was released shortly after I joined the B Wing community. At 2 p.m. that afternoon I was called down to the ground floor of the AU, my bags were packed and I made my way to what I was sure was going to be the hardest time of my life; I wasn't wrong.

B Wing is opposite the AU and holds some forty inmates and around a dozen staff. I was shown to my cell by the chairman and soon settled in. Many of the lads on the wing came up to introduce themselves, something never done in a normal prison where everyone has to fend for themselves. There were five groups on B Wing, each holding a maximum of eight men. I was allocated to Group 2 and for much of the next year the members of Group 2 were to share with me the good and bad times that lay ahead.

The first person I recognised on the wing was a man I had first met a few years earlier at Parkhurst and who was serving thirteen years for robbery; he was a very dangerous man whom I had seen stab two people in one day because they were late paying for their dope. I shall call him Sean, an Irishman in his late thirties. I made a mental note that I was going to have as little to do with him as possible. I did not need at that time to add to my own problems by mixing with people like him. My hopes were dashed when I discovered that not only was he a Group 2 member, he also occupied the cell right next door to mine.

The next shock was to find that I was allocated a Group 2 member as a 'sponsor', someone who has been in therapy a fair time and can be trusted to show a new member of the community the ropes. My sponsor, Gary, was a man I had first met in the Dolls' House at Winchester fifteen years before, who was now serving a life sentence for two rapes, the second of which he committed while on bail for the first. I was given a copy of the wing policies by the chairman – no drugs, sex or violence, no putting your feet on the furniture or watching television during the work periods, no missing groups or wings without a very good reason, and many more. One of the problems with the wing policies, I later discovered, was that there was no effective continuity. The policies were decided by the community as a whole, but they were not kept up to date and this often caused problems.

The therapy timetable looked like this:

MONDAY	2.45 p.m. to 3.45 p.m.	Community Meeting
TUESDAY	8.30 a.m. to 9.30 a.m.	Group Meeting
	9.30 a.m. to 10.15 a.m.	Feedback Session
WEDNESDAY	2.45 p.m. to 3.45 p.m.	Group Meeting
	3.45 p.m. to 4.15 p.m.	Feedback Session
THURSDAY	10.15 a.m. to 11.15 a.m.	Community Meeting
FRIDAY	2.45 p.m. to 3.45 p.m.	Group Meeting
	3.45 p.m. to 4.15 p.m.	Feedback Session

The system was designed so that work periods could be slotted in with therapy. B Wing had the same timetable as C

Wing, while D Wing and F Wing (for young offenders) had the opposite shift. This resulted in two wings working while the other two were doing therapy, and vice versa. I missed the first community meeting because I had just moved on to the wing and was still unpacking my belongings. The following morning, at the unearthly hour of 8.30, I had to attend my first group. I managed to avoid Sean for the first day, but there was no way I could avoid him on the group; it was a case of not having any more contact with him than I felt was necessary.

At teatime on my first day I was approached by a lad who had been on the AU with me and with whom I had smoked dope. He asked me if I wanted some dope and I agreed; no harm in a joint, is there? I was later to realise the foolishness of what I was doing. The policies of the wing also included what was termed therapeutic feedback – grassing is what anyone else would have called it. The rationale behind it, in the Grendon context, is not to make people grass on others, but to ensure a relaxed atmosphere in which therapy could take place. Each man comes to Grendon as a volunteer, and is accepted for therapy on the basis that he agrees in writing to comply with all of the rules and regulations which are inherent in a therapeutic regime. If a man came to Grendon for help with a drugs problem, then it was not helping him – or his next victim – if during his time at Grendon he continued to take drugs. There were also policies of no gossiping; prisons thrive on gossip and scandal. If a person breaks any of the policies fixed by the community, then other community members who see it either have to 'group' or 'wing' the person for it. The former means that the individual has to speak about what took place on his next group; if he fails to do so, then he has to face the community as a whole (winging). In the case of any breach of the major policies of the community, such as drugs, sex or violence, then it is an automatic winging and that can result, ultimately, in expulsion from Grendon and a return to the prison of origin.

It is a bewildering system when you are first thrust into it. Everyone is trying hard not to be 'grouped' and many see it as little more than an opportunity of disciplining those they dislike. I certainly saw it that way to begin with – no bloody prisoner was going to place me on report, that was for sure! But as I became involved in therapy I learnt to realise that these measures are of great importance. While it is tempting to see them as disciplinary measures, the objective is simply to get people to recognise where they are going wrong and give them the chance to discuss it and learn from it. The community could not have existed without grouping and winging and though, as I shall tell you, there were to be many times in the months ahead when I wished the damn things had never been invented, that was only sour grapes on my part for being caught doing things I should not have done.

My first group meeting took place the following morning. Being late for groups is not something to be recommended for you are not allowed to enter the group once it has started, but have instead to face the wing and explain why you were unable to attend. Being winged is not something for the faint of heart, for they are heated affairs in which a great deal of anger and frustration is vented. I made sure I was not late for my first group and found myself facing five other prisoners along with two members of staff, Ashley Lindsay (probation) and the irrepressible Joe Chapman, a basic-grade prison officer who had then been at Grendon for thirteen years. Because it was my first group there were introductions to be made, again by name, sentence and offence. Sean and Gary were both present and in addition I found there was Alan (serving life for buggery of a nine-year-old boy), Nick (serving thirteen years for a double rape of a seventy-year-old woman) and Peter (serving five years for GBH).

At the start of each group meeting there was a strict order to be followed. First, any jobs currently vacant are advertised. Any member of the group who wishes to apply for a job then has to explain to the group the therapeutic reasons for his application and persuade the group to support him. Some job applicants are not volunteers but are put forward by their respective group. Next come groupings. If any member of the group has been 'grouped' by another member of the community then he must discuss it as soon as jobs are out of the way; the person responsible for the grouping also has to inform his own group about it, and explain why he felt it was necessary.

After the introductions, jobs and groupings the group was used for the next hour by Alan. I took an immediate dislike to him and it remained with me for most of the time I knew him. He was thirty years old and had served twelve years of his life sentence; a sentence he specifically asked the judge to impose. He had been in and out of homes all his life and he gave me the impression of being a false person who hid his dangerousness behind a smiling face. (To some extent you have to read that through the eyes of someone who has suffered abuse and who finds it extremely difficult to have any time at all for those responsible for such things.)

Alan had received a letter from his father, the first time he had heard from him in ten years. He blamed his father for much of what had happened and saw him as being the cause of his offending. The group were not having that. As I sat back and listened to this bewildering system of therapy, I saw the group round on him. It was his fault for what he had done, he was old enough to know that it was wrong, it was no good simply blaming it on others; 'What about the victim?' Alan began to get upset, banging the arm of the chair in anger. He did not know what to do about the letter from his father and the group told him that he should reply and if possible arrange a visit. He kept trying to swing it around by saying that he really didn't want to know his father and he blamed everyone but himself for his offending. But B Wing Group 2 was probably the strongest group in Grendon at that time, certainly the one where the most 'work' was done, and they were having none of it. Joe Chapman, with whom I built up a very good relationship during the course of the following twelve months – and with whom I still correspond – was largely responsible for the group's good reputation and he tackled Alan about his father and his relationship. In the end Alan agreed to write and invite him to Grendon, even to have him sit in on a group meeting; but it was clear that this was really the last thing he wanted. One hour after it all began I heard the wing chairman shout 'feedback' and we all moved down to the wing television room to join the rest of the groups which had by then assembled there. One member of each group had the task of 'feeding back' to the rest of the community what had taken place on their respective group meeting.

Accordingly it is at Feedback that you learn who has applied for jobs, who has been grouped and what it was for – as well as who has been grouped but failed to mention it; an automatic winging! Then each group in turn, through the person doing feedback that day, informs the rest of the community what they have been up to for the last hour; who used the group, why and what was achieved. The chairman writes down the feedback from each group and records it in the Wing Book which is available to any member of the community simply by asking the chairman.

After the feedback was complete the rest of the morning was recreation time, but I went up to my cell, pushed the door to and wondered just what the hell I had let myself in for. I had never before been to a prison where prisoners were accountable to other prisoners for their behaviour and attitude. My world was turned upside down and I lay on my bed throughout the morning, still unsure about my commitment to see this through. Sean came in during the morning from his cell next door and told me that he had changed since we had last met at Parkhurst, but I put it down to nothing more than Irish blarney. I listened half-heartedly as he told me of his progress and I took it all with a pinch of salt. Only much later did I realise that he had been speaking the truth and, indeed, it was through watching and talking to Sean that I became convinced that Grendon can work where other institutions had failed.

Work did not really exist in Grendon. There were many workshops but they were all closed. There were essential work parties, such as kitchen and wing cleaners, the latter of whom were responsible not to a screw but to a foreman cleaner who was a prisoner able to deduct money if the standard of work was not what it should be. Each community (therapeutic wing) had representatives for tasks on the wing. There were reps for hygiene, video, games, television, information board, works (maintenance) and many more. Inmates held these jobs for three months at a time. Each job was designed to meet a particular therapeutic need: the TV rep, for example, was responsible for the nightly process of television votes. Because there was only one television in each community – on purpose for precisely this reason – the TV rep had to take votes each evening on what television programmes would be watched that night. Officially 'canvassing' for votes was not permitted and was a 'groupable' offence, but it still went on, much to the annoyance of those who could not abide 'EastEnders' or 'The Bill', but who were stuck with them twice a week! The job of TV rep would suit a person who, for example, found it difficult to mix within the community. This job thrust them into the community and forced them to take an active part in its running on a daily basis.

Once the applicants have been put forward the chairman has to fix a date for a job board at which each candidate is interviewed. This came as a shock. You had to be properly dressed as if you were going for a real interview – which you were – clean and smart and prepared to make out a case 'therapeutically speaking' as to why you should have the job in preference to any other candidate who had applied. The job board, as you have probably guessed, is staffed entirely by prisoners.

I have been through many job boards, both as a candidate and as a member of the selection panel. The panel of the job board is selected by the chairman who chooses one member from each group subject to that person having been in the community for three months. The chairman chairs each board, but has no vote other than a casting vote in the event of a tie. Strange as it may seem, I have always found that the job board was taken very seriously by the inmates, who tried hard to allocate the jobs on the basis of therapeutic need rather than nepotism. If a candidate had trouble mixing with others in the community he would be thought suitable to be placed in a job where he could not help but mix with others: TV rep for example, or foreman cleaner. If a person had a low tolerance level, prone to fits of temper when things did not go right, then he would be suitable to be placed in a job where his tolerance would be tested: serving the food, for example or, again, foreman cleaner. Conversely, if a candidate could not identify a therapeutic need for the job he had applied for, his chances of success were slim. There were no favourites and everyone was treated with the same degree of searching scrutiny. I found during my time at Grendon that this was by far the most thorough board that I have ever appeared in front of; proving once again that the hardest people to fool are your peers.

Shortly after I arrived on the wing, I was called in one morning to the staff group and invited to sign my treatment contract. This document sets out the wing policies and you are required to sign to the effect that you will abide by them, including that you will feed back to the wing or group anything you think they ought to know – irrespective of how difficult it may be to repeat. The wing psychologist, Roland Woodward – the image of Billy Connolly but not half as witty – witnessed my signature to the clauses and reminded me as I was leaving that I should make sure to abide by them, as he would make sure I was held to them; a promise he was to keep many times in the months ahead.

The community had a policy, I found out, that all new members had to spend their first two weeks behind the servery dishing out food and checking off names. This was a typical example of the Grendon philosophy of 'in at the deep end'. From the very first day the new member of the community is thrust forward, and made to play a full part. It prevented people from hiding away, and also ensured that by the end of the first week you knew every member of the community by name.

Joe Chapman was the first prison officer that I can say I ever really got along with – but I have to qualify that by saying that initially it was due more to his tolerance than any great change of attitude on my part. Joe was well liked by all, except some of the governor grades, for he has an ability to cut through red tape and bring pragmatic solutions to problems where others recognise only obstacles. If a person had a domestic problem at home, Joe would be concerned only with whether the partner was at home and able to talk on the telephone, rather than – like others – with the myriad official forms that had to be filled in before a telephone call could be made. That is not to say that he was an easy touch; he isn't and is more than capable of telling you in no uncertain terms where to go if he thinks you're having him over. He gave to me one day a piece of paper containing the following prose; it became very important to me as I tried to follow it with varying degrees of success. It comes, I believe, from Alcoholics Anonymous, though they tell me that it is not official AA literature and they believe the author, aptly, is anonymous.

Just For Today . . .

Just for today I will try to live through this day only and not tackle my whole life problems at once. I can do something for twelve hours that would appal me if I had to keep it up for a lifetime.

Just for today I will be happy. Most folks are as happy as they make up their minds to be.

Just for today I will adjust myself to what is, and not try to adjust everything to my own desires. I will take my 'luck' as it comes and fit it to myself.

Just for today I will try to strengthen my mind. I will learn something useful. I will not be a mental loafer. I will read something which requires effort and concentration.

Just for today I will exercise my soul in three ways: I will do somebody a good turn and *not* get found out. If anybody knows of it, it will not count. I will do at least two things that I do not want to do – just for exercise. I will not show anyone that my feelings are hurt; they may be hurt, but today I will not show it.

Just for today I will be agreeable. I will look as well as I can, dress becomingly, talk low, act courteously, criticise not one bit, not find fault with anything and try not to improve or regulate anybody but myself. Just for today I will have a programme. I may not follow it exactly, but I will have it. I will save myself from two pests: hurry and indecision. Just for today I will be unafraid. Especially I will not be afraid to enjoy what is beautiful and to believe that as I give to the world, so the world will give to me.

It is a tremendous task to stick to that, even for one day, but I used to read it each morning and at odd times during the day. I spent many hours talking to Joe and our relationship became the stronger for it. He is a man full of common sense and not beyond a practical joke either; his cartoons are excellent and should be entered for awards. Joe had been married twice when I first met him and is now into his third and, he assures me, his last marriage, to a lovely young lady called Wendy.

During my first two months I also had long chats with Sean. I watched him very carefully for I was acutely aware of how dangerous he was. I had to admit by the end of the second month that there had certainly been a change within him. He no longer growled at people but spoke to them in a rational way. His Irish sense of humour matured as time went by and he became a committed Christian. He also took up meditation and would spend hours in the group room sitting cross-legged on a little cushion away in a world of his own. During my first two months I changed my diet to become vegan because he showed me that I could lose weight by eating sensibly and cutting out all the food I loved! One evening the kitchen sent to the wing four packets of chocolate biscuits for the four vegans in the community, but they contained animal fats. Sean absolutely refused to have his principles compromised, though I have to admit that I was happy to munch away my packet – and his as well; such is life!

I started to jog around the exercise yard each day and the weight began to fall off. Believe me, it was sheer pleasure to break that twelve-stone barrier. I enjoyed my hour of jogging for it provided me with the opportunity of being alone with my thoughts and I found it a useful way of burning off the frustrations which still raged within me at being thrust into this alien environment and regime that I found hard to accept. Yes, I wanted to go straight on my release, but I had not bargained for this kind of regime as a route to get there. Strangely, however, as the weeks went by, I became more and more aware that I was committed to this changing process. Grendon is a harsh regime. There is no hiding away from your faults for there are forty people only too happy to point them out to you; they are displayed for all to see and discuss. For me, with my rapidly diminishing aura of being high and mighty, I found the changing process exceptionally difficult, but I knew without it I was destined to spend the rest of my life in one type of penal regime or another.

I had been in B Wing for just two months when I received my first grouping by another inmate. Tuesday morning is set aside for early groups, followed by feedback and then the collection of wages. The canteen at Grendon is a small room at the top of the long M1 corridor. As a consequence only six inmates at a time are able to attend and new ones are despatched as old ones return. I came out of feedback one Tuesday morning to find that a long queue was waiting at the wing door to go to the canteen. John Keen, the wing senior officer, was standing at the gate and letting people in as others came back. Well, I thought, I'm not going to wait around like a lemon. I went to the front of the queue and told the officer that I was going to the library which, conveniently, was situated next door to the canteen. Three minutes later I was standing in the canteen queue, quite pleased with my little bit of deception. Alas, I should have known better.

The very first person to come around the corner – going legitimately to the canteen – was Alan, the person on my group I disliked a great deal and felt was false. He had heard me say that I was going to the library and so came about my first grouping for 'being devious' as he put it. Of all the bloody cheek! I felt embarrassed and humiliated that I had been caught out and tried to defend myself on the spot by having a go at him. I poured out all the bad things I could think of and hurled them at him. To my absolute dismay he refused to bite and that only made my anger more heated. The following afternoon I reported to my group that I had been grouped and explained the circumstances – which in reality was a version of events twisted in my favour. I learnt a very painful lesson that afternoon, you cannot kid the people who have themselves spent a lifetime kidding others.

The group tore into me and slagged me down. We went at each other hammer and tongs and I felt hatred for the prisoners who were supposed to be on my side but who insisted on siding with others – including screws. I batted off every criticism that they bowled at me and steadfastly refused to budge from my position that Alan had misheard me saying I was going to the library; I was giving them bullshit and what's more they knew it. The strength of Grendon is that the prisoners will not easily let one of their number off the hook. They see it as just as much a part of their therapy to point out your mistakes, as it is for you to point out theirs – and you have to listen to each other. Joe Chapman said little during the meeting and just sat there and watched as I dug a bigger and bigger hole for myself. As I left the room that day he made his one and only comment of the afternoon, 'Mark, why do you have such a problem handling rejection?' It stopped me dead in my tracks. The problem was not that I had deceived John Keen on the gate, nor that I had jumped the queue in front of others who were prepared to wait their turn. That was bad enough. The underlying problem was that I could not handle being caught out and did everything in my power to get out of it. I stormed off and missed the feedback. I lay on my bed, my emotions churning over and over and I realised I was reaching the stage where I had to go forward and make the jump into therapy – or leave.

After tea that evening I called a special group. This is a procedure whereby a person can call together his group for a special meeting outside of normal therapy times to discuss something which needs to be talked through and cannot really wait until the next scheduled group meeting. Therapy comes first in Grendon. Meetings are more important than anything else, and when a special group is called you are required to attend. We met in the quiet room on the wing, normally the place reserved for board games, and were all seated around in a circle. I poured out all the frustrations that had been building up within me. Grendon caused me tremendous conflict. I had never been in a system before where prisoners sided with authority. To me it was against everything I had ever believed in. I knew I had been wrong and I apologised to Alan for the verbal lashing I had given him. I had acted deceitfully and had been caught out; that was not his problem, it was mine. Rejection was at the very root of my problems and that day I made the decision to start working on it. I knew that it would not be easy and could not be changed overnight. I had to begin to amend my behaviour and that involved others telling me when I was going wrong and, equally important, my having the balls to accept it and do something about it.

I came out of that two-hour meeting feeling much better with myself and the group rallied round once they realised that I was prepared to work towards change. Slowly the defects in my character began to dawn on me. I did have problems handling rejection and it had been an integral part of my life; I knew the problem, but not the answer. That was supplied by Sean, who said, quite simply, 'It's not a case of being able to handle rejection, Mark, it's a matter of amending your attitude and behaviour so that people have no need to reject you in the first place.' Simple and to the point as ever.

My head was 'in bits', as they say, that night as I struggled with the new information that was being forced into my resisting brain. The criminal code of behaviour that I had so long subscribed to, all the beliefs that I had been taught, were slowly being exposed as bullshit; it was another devastating experience along the painful road of reform. From that point on I went out of my way to mix with others on the wing. I climbed down off my high horse and attempted to speak to others without allowing thoughts of their offences to act as a barrier. I joined the wing football team, even though I was not much good at it, and played rugby for the prison; very slowly I was moving towards becoming what in Grendon is known as a 'theraputon'. That was when Ian came up to me.

Ian is a lifer, sentenced for the murder of his gay lover. Thin as a beanpole and prematurely bald, he was a real character. As camp as they come and as witty as you will find, he suggested to me that we do a 'Hinge and Bracket' sketch for the forthcoming social evening. Well, I was not too sure about that, but what the hell, anything to brighten up the atmosphere. He drafted out a script and we persuaded our only female officer, Julie Briggs, to donate for the evening some of her clothes.

B Wing community hosted a social evening every four months. Inmates on the wing contributed ten pence per week from their wages to a fund for a buffet, which they also prepared – supervised by the inevitable social rep. We were allowed to invite 'professional people' who could come along for a bit of Home Office propaganda and a bite to eat. The Hinge and Bracket travesty went off a treat, lasting about twenty minutes. It was a pretty amateurish performance by any standards, but it brightened up the evening and gave everyone a good laugh. The chairman introduced us by denying 'any responsibility for what is about to occur'. The sketch was loaded with sexual innuendos and even the governor thought it hilarious.

Though things in the wing were getting better I was reminded shortly after the social evening that I was at Grendon for therapy; and I belonged to a vigilant group. I went along one evening as a candidate on a job board, applying for full-time education. I had applied through my group the previous week and had received their backing. In retrospect I should have realised that something was amiss because they agreed to it far too easily for Group 2, who normally scrutinised all such job applications thoroughly to make sure there was a valid therapeutic reason. On the board from my group was Nick, the young black guy serving thirteen years for double rape. He had even said to me when vacancies on full-time education were advertised that I should 'go for it', so I thought I had one vote in the bag before the curtain went up!

When I sat down in the hot seat in front of the job board, I very quickly discovered that Nick was going to go out of his way to make sure that I did not get the job – and he was far more successful than I was. I came out of the board hot with anger and flew up to his cell to have it out with him. He listened while I poured out all the verbal abuse I could think of and then he simply said, 'The group told you a week ago that you had not learnt to handle rejection. The fact that you are here ranting and raving like a lunatic proves the point: discuss it on the group.' I had not only failed to get the job and been grouped in the process, I had also been set up and had fallen for it. Shit!

Therapy is an on-going thing and, tempting as it may be to rest on your laurels, that is dangerous. When the group next met I had to speak about what had happened after the job board. I had learned to some extent that it was no use trying to pull the wool over their eyes with a load of excuses; what mattered most was where I had gone wrong. Joe Chapman said that in his view it was a case of 'setting up my own rejection' – which I thought was a load of rubbish until I gave it some thought. There was no reason for me to apply for full-time education. Yes, I wanted to progress in legal studies, but I had come to Grendon to change my way of life. I could have gone to any prison in the country to advance my education, but there was in reality no therapeutic reason for applying for the job in the first place. By asking the group to back me, I was asking them to agree to something which they should not have been asked to do and they decided to teach me a lesson – again. I was learning all the time, but it was difficult to try to keep these lessons at the forefront of your mind each minute of the day as you went about your business. I tried hard after that to remain aware of what I was doing and to a large extent I achieved it. But around the corner danger lurked and I was to be placed in a position where my commitment to therapy was to be tested to the full.

'Compromise' is a word you hear a great deal in the Grendon therapeutic regime. It is the devil of therapy and slowly eats away at progress and prevents further advances being made. It comes about when one person has a 'hold' over another person and neither can progress as a result. I had smoked dope once while a member of the B Wing community and if that were discovered I would lose my place and have to return to Dartmoor. Only one other person – Len – knew that I had smoked and so I thought that I was safe from being exposed. But as time went on I soon realised that *I* knew and that was more than enough. I had signed to say I would not do it and as long as Len knew about it, I had a hold over him, just as much as he had a hold over me. I had come to Grendon to change and although smoking dope in the community actually went on quite a lot, though in small circles, the time was very quickly approaching when I knew I would have to make real decisions about changing *my* life.

One morning at 8.30 the community was called to a special wing meeting and assembled in the television room. Special wing meetings – as distinct from special groups – were very rare occasions; there were only two during the whole time I was in Grendon. This morning as we were assembled in the television room we heard the sound of dogs and soon learnt that the wing was being swept by dogs trained to sniff out drugs. I was confident that I was clean, but as I looked around the room I saw many people looking anxiously at each other. The result was that the dogs discovered a joint – cannabis cigarette – hidden in one of Len's speakers in his cell, and gave the impression to their handlers that drugs had been smoked in a large number of other cells in which no drugs had actually been located. Len had to face the wing for having the joint in his cell and his place at Grendon was on the line.

The wing met the next day to hear the case and he was invited to give his account of what the joint was doing in the back of his speaker. His response was to say that he had placed it there a year ago while at another prison and had completely forgotten about it. He denied having smoked drugs while at Grendon, though at least a dozen knew full well that he had and, from the fairly mild questioning, it was clear that many others on the wing were in a similar position; none of us dared contradict him in case he turned round and pointed out that he had smoked with us. The majority of people in that room knew that he was talking a load of crap but there were very few people who could have spoken out without committing therapeutic suicide.

Those who could have done so, myself included, were prevented from doing so by the need to protect our own positions; in Grendonspeak we were all 'compromised'. A vote was taken – from which I abstained – on whether Len should stay and it was overwhelmingly in his favour. I left that room with my mind in turmoil and went upstairs to my cell. On the way Len passed me on the stairs and asked me why I had abstained. I told him that he knew as well as I did that he had been speaking a load of rubbish. If he didn't want to do therapy and sort himself out then he should let someone else in the system have his place. He looked at me as if I was out of my head. 'I enjoy a smoke and a toot,' he told me. 'But your victim proves that you can't control it, Len,' I responded. I left him on his own to think about it. We had all sat and listened for an hour and a half to complete and utter bollocks and not one person had the courage to contradict him. Either I could go on fooling myself or I could make the decision which I knew had to be made and remove this very great fetter that was preventing me from moving forward; I'd reached the water-shed.

I had found it easy to kid myself that all I had to do was say nothing and no one would be any the wiser. But the problem went much deeper than that. I was marking out a pathway for myself in life; relying on not being caught seemed to me to be without sense at all. Our prisons are jammed to the rooftops with prisoners who deluded themselves they would not get caught. I had never faced such a difficult decision before in my life. It was something which went to the very core of the criminal codes of behaviour which I had always subscribed to but was in the process of discarding: you admit to nothing and deny everything.

The next morning I went to see Sean who had just been elected wing chairman and I booked a minute on the wing that afternoon. No one ever promised me that change would be easy or a bed of roses. I had come to Grendon to change and I did so like everyone else in the full and certain knowledge that it was a hard road along which sacrifices would have to be made; I was committed and there was no going back. I knew full well that it would cause trouble, that it would create all kinds of problems and divisions and would undoubtedly throw up more than I had bargained for, but the time had come to discard the criminal codes which had ruled my life so far, along with all the twisted myths and legends.

An hour or so before the meeting assembled I went to see Len and told him that I was going to do something he might find very hard to accept, but I was doing it because it had to be done and I did not want anyone to say later that they didn't know what was happening. I was going to admit that while I had been on B Wing I had smoked and it would then be for others to do their bit if they wanted. In a way I think he was relieved. Drugs had played a large part in his offending. He had caused horrific injuries to a girl while on drugs and he, like me, said that he had come to Grendon to change his way of life; he was not achieving that as long as he continued to smoke dope and snort smack. There was no animosity between us and he realised that what was happening was nothing more than what everyone in the community had promised to do as a result of signing their treatment contract, but had lacked the resolve to do when push came to shove.

By the time the meeting assembled everyone knew what was going to happen and in a way I'm pleased they did because there were quite a few moments when my resolve was on the edge of weakening. The chairman asked for minutes and everyone looked at me to see whether I would have the balls to go through with it, and I did. I said that since coming to Grendon I had smoked dope on the AU and once on B Wing, that I felt the time had come to make it known that I wasn't into drugs any longer, and if as a result of owning up I lost my place, then that would have to be the result, but I would go out with my head held high knowing that I had done something which others in the community found too hard to do. I said that I knew there were others who smoked on the wing and were unable to speak out, but the only way of doing something positive while they were here was to stand up and admit that they – like me – had fucked up. There was total silence. Forty people stared at me and then, to my absolute astonishment, four hands went up, one of which belonged to our new wing chairman, Sean. In Grendonspeak, we had a drugs scandal!

I knew of course that I would have to face the wing and explain what I had done and that my place at Grendon was on the line. Going on the wing was not a prospect I viewed with any great sense of alarm. I had made my decision and it was now too late to be worried about the consequences. After the meeting closed the group was roughly split into two camps, but there was no going back. I had signed the contract and I would abide by it and not pay lip-service to it; there had to be more to therapy than that. Many people afterwards sought me out and said they were pleased someone had the balls to reveal what was going on. Later I was told I would be facing the community the following week. There had been no whispered conversations behind closed doors, that was not my style – I said what I had to say and in front of everyone. Now I would stand or fall by it.

On the day of the winging I learnt that Len had put his papers in, that is, pulled out of therapy and requested a move back into the prison system. I felt genuinely sad about that because he did have a problem handling drugs and, unless he could work on that problem and come to terms with it, it was simply a prescription for more victims further down the road. I spoke to him before I had to face the wing and he was quite philosophical about leaving. He said that he had wanted to speak out himself but had never found the courage to do so. I told him that it was not too late for him and he could do whatever he wished. His future was in his own hands, not mine. He left Grendon shortly after and returned to Lewes prison in Sussex. I heard a year or so later that he had been found dead from a drug overdose in the Charing Cross area of London but I have never been able to confirm that.

When the wing met that afternoon I admitted again that I had smoked while I had been at Grendon and for the next hour I answered honestly all the questions asked of me. I explained that I had smoked dope for at least a decade and could not see that for me there was any particular problem with it. I was reminded that the call to Mountain Rescue had been made while I was high on dope, but it could equally have been made while I was drunk on drink; it wasn't the dope that caused it, but my own mentality. I saw no particular reason why I shouldn't smoke it, but I accepted that while I was at Grendon there were people present who had very great problems handling it and if I was to help them with their problems – since I expected them to help me with mine – then I had to give it up. I had not done that and the least I could do was to be honest about it and hope that those others who smoked and did have a drug problem would do the same; then perhaps we could all get down to doing what we were there for. I was asked if I would smoke dope when I was released and I answered quite honestly that I most probably would. I enjoyed a smoke, it gave me a very pleasant feeling and made me happy. But while I was at Grendon I would not smoke and I would not expect others to do so either.

I explained to everyone present that I fully intended to abide by my treatment contract and in future if any person offered me drugs of any kind then they would have to explain it to their group and then the community as a whole. We simply had to get away from the situation where people were prevented from doing the one thing which they had volunteered for: therapy. If they wished to smoke dope that was fine by me, all I asked was that they went back into the system and did it, giving their place to someone who would make better use of it. They had volunteered just like I had and if they did not like it then they – like me – were 'free' to leave Grendon at any time they chose. But that meant that as long as they remained at Grendon they should abide by their contract and do the therapeutic work they had signed an agreement to do. It certainly gave them something to think about.

The result was that I was voted by the community to stay – unanimously. The decision was relayed to the staff group the following week when they met to consider the case. The vote of the inmate community acts only as a recommendation to the staff group who have the right of veto. In my case they agreed with the inmate vote and from that point on I was able to get down to dealing with the very real problems I still had not covered on my group: sexual abuse, its effects on me as a person, and my ultimate sexual orientation. I was also aware that after that meeting people on the wing saw me in a different way. They respected what I had done in bringing drug taking into the open and I realised that I would now have to live up to their expectations; but there were also people who were waiting for me to fall, and fail.

On the group I began to work on the sexual abuse: what had caused it, why did it happen, what effects did it have on me and was there any connection between that and my ultimate sexual orientation. On my group were a number of prisoners who had been guilty of child sexual abuse and I found it very difficult to explain just what long-term effects that type of behaviour has on their victims. I had enormous problems at first even discussing it with them, but we were all there to learn and if I could prevent one more child from going through the horror of abuse as I had done, then speaking to them about it was a small price to pay, and was just as much a part of my therapy as it was a part of theirs.

I learnt from listening to them that they always believed that their victims were in agreement with what they were doing, but that is to invest a child with far more understanding than they possess. Children do not seek sexual abuse and I defied any of them to come up with one single piece of evidence to support it. Children depend on adults for their care and well being, and they seek love, warmth and protection, none of which is compatible with abuse. It is no answer to counter that they did not complain about it or talk about it to others; even at a young age children 'know' that sexual abuse is wrong. For many years I could not stand being touched even in a totally innocent way. I would shy away from people who were no threat to me, but whose actions – in putting their arms around me for example – made me go cold. It created within me deep-seated feelings of mistrust and was ultimately responsible for an anti-authority attitude that I still to some extent carry with me.

To lie prone while someone uses and abuses your body in the guise of 'love' has to be experienced to be understood. I was unable to speak about it to anyone, not only because I believed I would be sent 'home' from Lakeview, but also because I knew that no one would believe it was happening. In the late 1960s sexual abuse was not recognised in any great way, and the results of Cleveland reveal that it was not until the late 1980s that people began to realise just how wide-spread it was. It damaged my life for the best part of twenty years, ruined the relationship with my family because I believed they were somehow responsible for it by sending me away, and it had a very great effect on my sexuality, though not, I believe, on my ultimate orientation. That was also a point covered on the group and one which I had often thought about – was the abuse responsible for my being homosexual? I have to conclude that it was not; I know many people who have suffered abuse but who, at least from a sexual point of view, remain heterosexual.

In my view our sexuality is defined within us from birth very much like the colour of our eyes. I do not say that it cannot be shaped to some extent by sexual experiences (I believe that it can), but I cannot accept that it can be fundamentally altered; it is too basic a characteristic of our personality. We are born with different tastes in many respects, ranging from the colours we like to the aromas we cannot abide. There may be no rational reason for these, but they cannot be changed simply because they are unfashionable, or not socially accept-able. No amount of therapy will alter our inherent tastes. We are what we are. No matter how much we like or dislike it, we are stuck with it and have to make the best of it. What cannot be changed – as they say at Grendon – has to be accepted.

The discussion of all these issues could not have taken place without a basic foundation of trust within the group. It took months of work for that trust to develop, but it was the strength of the group therapy regime. Without trust a group could not work, and I recognised that many times in other groups who did not achieve anywhere near the level of therapeutic work that Group 2 did. It is for that reason that I have not written to any great extent about the therapy of other individuals at Grendon. They are entitled to their privacy, and while I may be prepared to discuss my problems I accept and respect that they may not share my views.

I continued on B Wing to attend the life skills group run by Annette Tyler from the AU. Slowly our relationship did improve and I saw her in a different light as my own problems began to be dealt with. The life skills group was a great help to me in many ways. I discovered that the wearing of the naval uniform was because I had never had status in my life. I had been in too many institutions for too many years where I was considered to be nothing more than a convict, and the naval uniform was instant, if dishonest, status.

In mid-October 1989 I went along to the prison library, as I did once every week. As prison libraries go, Grendon was one of the finest I have seen but it was only open once a week and so time and care had to be taken when selecting books that could not be changed for another seven days. There is nothing more annoying than reading almost a whole book only to discover that some idiot short of a cigarette paper has chosen the climax page as a substitute rizla. The officer on duty in the library, an ex-Royal Marine who made it perfectly clear that he was posted to Grendon and had no interest in the work that it did, was tutting away in the background as I was the only one left. Previously I would have delayed and delayed to annoy him, but I had learnt that there were better ways of doing things and after all I already had selected five of my six books. I reached out and took the first book to hand, *How to Write Radio*

Drama, and returned to my cell. Four days later when I put down my pen I had written my first-ever play for radio and discovered the sheer beauty that comes from stringing words together. In its initial form the play was not so much lamentable as potentially libellous, but it was a courtroom drama (what else?) with a good story and a strong plot and despite its failings I was delighted with it.

There was no stopping me after that. All the frustrations of therapy were taken out by using the pen and I wrote and wrote. I went through A4 writing pads faster than the Home Office go through roof tiles and I stared at a VDU until I was green in the face – and I loved every minute of it. Like Jimmy Boyle with his discovery of sculpture, I had found a legitimate outlet for my energies, which I enjoyed tremendously, which enabled me to achieve something good, and which, if others are to be believed, I'm not too bad at! I spent many hours typing up the play, 'The Facts Speak for Themselves', and after three re-writes sent it to the BBC as a 90-minute Saturday Night Theatre – it was accepted! I also entered the play for the 1990 Koestler Awards, a national competition each year for prisoners in the UK, where it won a prize of £20; we all have to start somewhere!

On 15 November 1989 I was approached by a member of the community called Russell, a Glaswegian with an infectious amount of enthusiasm, serving seven years for robbery. He asked whether I would write a Christmas pantomime which he hoped to put on in aid of local handicapped children; I was only too pleased to accept and started work that day. When 'The "Other" Dick Whittington' was completed two weeks later it had a running time of an hour and a quarter and a cast of about twenty. Set in the late nineteenth century it concerned the antics of Dick Whittington and his friend Pussy. Dick, a kind and caring chap, had a double – known appropriately as Double Dick – who was devious and, had he been around today, would have spent a good number of years on the Ghostrain. He was responsible for stealing the wallet of a Mr

Toogood, who identified Dick Whittington as the culprit. That resulted in Dick making an appearance before Mr Justice Grumberly-Guts, charged with theft, along with Pussy who was nicked for trying to foil Mr Whittington's arrest; his loyal shouts to the arresting PC Catchalot, 'Take your hands off my Dick!' went down in Grendon history. The jury were hopelessly Tory, paid-up members of the hang-'em-flog-'em committee, so the verdict of guilty was never much in doubt; despite the antics of the drunken prosecution witness, the Right Reverend, Reverend Wright, who appeared under the impression that he had been nicked for being drunk. Justice was finally done when Double Dick was nicked with the wallet and the two innocents released.

Russell and myself took great pains to get it right and interested a large number of staff in the project. John Keen, the wing senior officer I had deceived with my trip to the library, bore no grudges and was a great help, coming in during his days off with his tools to help build the scenery; a rare man, John Keen. Joe Chapman was also willing to help and within a month we were ready to put on the play. We had squeezed a £200 costume budget out of Mike Lambe, Grendon's education officer – himself a published playwright – acquired use of the gymnasium and had timber for the scenery donated by a certain company in the town who gave us the Jewson lot! Invitations were sent and B Wing community were a great help in rescheduling their programme to facilitate our rehearsals. The play was not intended for children themselves, but for adults we hoped could be persuaded to dig deep in aid of the handicapped; the date was fixed for 23 December, with a second showing the following week for the inmates. As we approached the date there was a great feeling that we were really achieving something worthwhile and staff had already been persuaded (or was it press-ganged?) into coughing up £100. But our plans were to be dashed as a result of something we could never have foreseen in a million years.

On the afternoon of 20 December 1989, the wing was called to a special meeting at 5 p.m.; only the second during my stay at Grendon. I knew it was a serious matter when I noted that the wing principal officer, Bob Manning, was present; he had never attended any of the meetings before. Sean had been summoned to see the governor along with all the other wing chairmen and as he strode into the television room at 5 p.m. he said, 'It's not as bad as you all thought it was – it's worse. Grendon closes down as from tomorrow.' There was total silence. The trouble was caused by electrical problems. A firm of consultants had been called in to check the wiring and found the buildings were a death trap. They produced a damning report which landed on the desk of governor Michael Selby that afternoon and within a short time the decision had been taken to shut the prison down completely and evacuate everyone.

In just eight months Grendon had become very precious to me. It was more than a prison to me and I felt very attached to it; once again the world seemed to be crashing down around my ears and I was helpless to prevent it. People were walking around in a stupor that evening, unable to quite believe what was happening. The staff allowed everyone telephone calls to inform their relatives what was taking place. I know of no other long-term prison that could have been evacuated as quickly without a single disciplinary incident along the way. That spoke volumes about the resilience of Grendon; and the fact that it was successfully transplanted – twice – is further evidence of its intrinsic value.

I was devastated; there was no other word for it. There were rumours that some would be going to Winchester prison and the rest to a young offender institution which was not yet fully opened: the Mount, in Hemel Hempstead. I was not happy at the prospect of going back into the system, and arriving in a convoy from Grendon would not create the best of entrances. People around me were convinced, as I was, that this was the end of Grendon, the experiment was over and the inmates were to be discarded around the penal system. It was all too much for me. I had come to believe in a new way of doing things and I felt a tremendous sadness that we appeared to have reached the end of the road. I went up on the landings as everyone was slowly packing their belongings, taking posters off the wall or simply sitting in their cells unable to believe that this – just three days before the night of the panto – was actually taking place. Shortly after 7 p.m. I found I was one of twenty-nine selected for HMP Winchester. To me that meant only one thing: Dartmoor. I was shell-shocked.

I walked about the wing that evening and watched the people who had shared my good and bad times. I cared for them in a way that I had never cared collectively for prisoners in the past. They had trusted me enough to share their most private thoughts with me and I had done the same in return; I felt completely drained. I sat with those who were going to Winchester with me the following morning and it was generally agreed that it was over. The staff were saying Grendon would be reopened in six months, but we were all convinced that they were being fed bullshit from above in an effort to make our departure as orderly as possible. When I saw the dope being brought out I didn't really know what to do. We were all in a state of limbo, and if that sounds like an excuse to justify what then took place – you're right.

After the first joint the concerns seemed to evaporate and when the doors closed at 9 p.m. I lay on my bed and looked at Eddie the Eagle, my pet budgie, given to me by Pat and Arthur on one of their visits. Pat's name for him – Edwin – had been quickly amended to Eddie, and, after displaying a fondness for soaring around the cell whenever he was let out of his cage he had become known as Eddie the Eagle. He was a great little companion, and brought me many hours of pleasure at Grendon. I wondered what the immediate future held in store for us.

That night as the dope wore off I knew that I had been tested and found wanting. There were no excuses to offer.

'Therapy' was a way of life and did not come to an end simply because the prison had done so. I rebuked myself for my failure and though I was able to take comfort from the fact that the circumstances were unique, it was just not good enough. I had failed and I would talk about that failure and learn the lessons from it. The staff themselves had been in a quandary, too. At least I knew where I was going – they didn't have a clue where they were destined to be posted, just five days before Christmas.

I had my 'therapy head' back on in the morning, I awoke long before they opened my door and just lay there soaking up the quiet morning sunshine. Eddie was chirping away in his cage and I wondered what was to become of him. Winchester was a local prison and they do not allow inmates to have budgies. I had grown very fond of him and I didn't want to leave him behind. I would have to see if anything could be done about it, but the prospects were not good.

Breakfast was a dismal affair. There was no laughter and little talking. I went around the wing removing the posters which only twenty-four hours earlier had been proudly promoting the panto. The wing had changed from a happy unit of people all pulling together as a group to one where no one knew what was going to happen. The lifers were the first to leave and we (Group 2) held a special group to say our farewells to those members who were leaving us bound for D Hall at Wormwood Scrubs. I felt really sorry for them as they left; Wormwood Scrubs is not the best of places to spend Christmas.

All of my kit was packed and ready when I was told by Ted Cole, the deputy governor, that he had been in touch with Winchester and had persuaded the governor there to allow us to keep our belongings – including budgies. I was delighted. I was told that some of the Grendon staff would be posted to Winchester and the intention was to keep everyone together. Joe Chapman had been off sick and did not know of the closure until I managed to telephone him at home to break the news. He had been a great help to me and I did not want to leave without thanking him for his help. That afternoon twenty-nine of us boarded a coach – complete with police outriders – and were taken to Winchester. As the gates of Grendon closed behind me, I looked back and wondered when I would be seeing them again; in my heart I think I knew it was the last time.

When we arrived at the reception of Winchester prison that evening, we found that in addition to us there were also the prisoners returning from the courts to be processed; it was going to be a long night. I sat down and wondered what the future held. Grendon is known as a nuthouse and it was common knowledge that it held a large number of sexual offenders. Many of those who came to Winchester fell into that category and we decided amongst ourselves that we would not identify them to other inmates. While I was seated in reception an officer approached and informed me that they had dropped Eddie's cage while unloading the bus and had smashed the top. He was fine but from the noise he was making he was not too pleased with the damage.

That evening we were all dotted around the prison and it was strange to be sharing a cell again. John, my cell mate, was not from B wing in Grendon and so we had to go through the process of getting to know each other; we were up until about 4 a.m. talking about what had happened and where we thought we would be sent. The following morning I came out of the cell to find that there were quite a few people around I knew from other prisons, and they were quite taken aback when I refused the dope they offered me! In the afternoon I discovered that two of the Grendon lads on another wing had been threatened and the governor decided to clear a landing and keep us all together. Within twenty-four hours of arrival – and for the duration of our stay – it was obvious that there was a tension in the air throughout the prison and the appalling conditions did little to reduce it.

The staff at Winchester did not like the idea of us being

treated differently and some of them went out of their way to prime other prisoners to cause trouble. Fortunately I knew many people in Winchester and their destructive efforts came to nothing. The staff from Grendon did not immediately materialise as promised and the lads were getting uptight. I was lying on my bed a few days later when the door opened and in walked Joe Chapman – what a sight for sore eyes. He brought with him another officer from Grendon called Derek, whom I had never met, and B wing's doctor, Roger Cruickshank; a man for whom I have little time and even less respect. However, it looked as if things were going to be okay and Joe persuaded the governor of Winchester to allow him to run the landing as if we were still at Grendon. We decided to hold wing meetings and to my surprise I found myself elected as the chairman of the Grendon-in-Winchester branch!

A good many of the lads were anxious over what was going to happen and the meetings were opportunities to discuss this and to find out news from the small number of Grendon governor grades who paid us a visit. According to Ted Cole, the plans were for us to remain at Winchester for about a month, when we would be moved to another prison at Wellingborough which was being cleared out. Wellingborough – or Grendonborough as it became known almost instantly – was a young offender institution near Northampton, and it spoke a great deal about the priority the regional director attributed to Grendon that he was willing, in the space of a month, to clear that establishment and make way for a reformed and transplanted Grendon Underwood.

I asked Mike Lambe, Grendon's education officer who visited us one day, whether his department could fund me on a professional writing course that I had seen advertised in the national press. He was aware that I had really taken to 'this writing lark', as he put it, and, being a playwright himself, he agreed. I was really looking forward to getting the course and learning what I knew would be my future 'trade' in life; I had 'opinions to peddle' as a certain robust circuit judge was later to put it.

As chairman of the wing I found it very difficult to maintain a sense of proportion about it all. I had my own worries and problems, and was then suddenly bestowed with those of twenty-eight others as well. There were one or two incidents during the time we were at Winchester, but not one disciplinary report. Joe Chapman did an excellent job and made our stay there as easy as was possible under the circumstances. The rest of the lads from Grendon, with the exception of the lifers who had gone to Wormwood Scrubs, had been sent to the Mount and by all accounts they were finding the transition difficult. There had been one suicide attempt involving a cell fire and a number of disciplinary reports.

Joe Chapman got us extra exercise periods and also arranged through the education officer at Winchester, David Davies, for us to use the education department one or two days a week. Gradually we did settle down and the daily meetings were a great help, allowing me to keep everyone updated with news of what was happening elsewhere. Just when we thought things were going well, I was told by Joe Chapman that news had come through that not all of the Winchester Twenty-Nine would be going to Wellingborough.

It seemed the staff at Wellingborough objected very much to their young offenders being turfed out and had been informing the local residents that all kinds of nutters would soon be prowling around their back gardens and threatening everything from their homes to their loved ones; complete rubbish, of course. The result of this misinformation was that a number of local residents, primed by the Wellingborough branch of the Prison Officers' Association (POA), complained through their member of Parliament and thereby brought pressure to bear on the Home Office. The minister instructed the regional director that no one was to be moved from Winchester to Wellingborough without having been the subject of an individual security vetting; Wellingborough was a closed establishment, security category C.

The selection process and security vetting were to take place at Grendon and Joe Chapman and his colleagues were invited to attend. Joe had written an individual report on everyone at Winchester and was of the view that everyone should be allowed to go to Wellingborough; it was clear, however, that there would have to be scapegoats in order to satisfy local residents. Joe gave each of us a copy of the report he would be presenting to the security meeting at Grendon. As I write this I have my copy to hand and it is interesting to read if only because it charts the distance covered since the governor of Dartmoor had called me a 'thoroughly offensive, dangerous and disruptive man'. This is what Joe Chapman wrote:

CF1449 LEECH, M.F. (B WING)

I have known this man since he began his therapy in B Wing, in fact I am his Group Officer. When he first came to Winchester I had expected him to take on the system as he has done in the past. To my surprise he has done exactly the opposite. He has been elected Wing Chairman by the other inmates and has been a great help to staff and a calming influence on the inmates. He is a mainstay of the B Wing Community, a man who has made excellent progress in therapy and who is destined to make a great success of his life. His record proves that Grendon Underwood can and does work.

Joe Chapman
Officer Gv.iii

The result of the Grendon security board was relayed to us the day following the meeting and, as expected, sacrifices had been made on the political altar. The campaigning work of Joe Chapman had, however, reduced this to just three inmates, but they understandably found it very difficult to accept. I was delighted to discover that I was going to Wellingborough, but later events were to reveal that I might as well have been one of those refused entry.

One day we were visited by Ashley Lindsay, the B Wing probation officer and a member of Group 2. I had not got along with Ashley at all during my first few weeks on B Wing, but we had come to know each other quite well and later had built up a good relationship. Ashley had been sexually abused as a child and that created a special bond between us because we had both experienced the same kinds of emotional problems. Ashley told me that he was leaving prison probation because he had been promoted to senior probation officer, and would thereafter be working in Cheshunt. I was pleased for him in many ways, but saddened that Group 2 would be losing a respected member who would be sorely missed. I spoke to Ashley about the night that Grendon closed down and particularly about why I had taken to dope when the first real test came along. He said it was understandable in the circumstances and I should discuss it with the group when we were all together again. I was sad to see him leave; Grendon's loss was Cheshunt's gain.

On 8 February 1990, twenty-six of us left by coach for Northampton. The three who had been denied entry to Wellingborough had already left, two going to Pentonville and one to Bristol. We arrived at Wellingborough late in the afternoon and very soon found ourselves back in the swing of things. Wellingborough had been taken over almost entirely by Grendon, though there were two wings given over to non-Grendon inmates with whom we had very little contact.

It was good to be back in a relaxed atmosphere among old friends and before very long it was almost as if we had never left. I lay on my bed that night after a hectic day in which we had been catching up on news and events since we had last all been together. Eddie was chirping away in his cage, pleased to be away from the noise of Winchester, while I was already replanning the panto! The following morning was groups as usual; we had had our break and now it was back to the therapeutic grindstone. I took the opportunity of discussing the smoking I had taken part in the night Grendon closed. Eighty per cent of the wing had been smoking on that crazy night, but feedback revealed that only five of us had admitted to it during the groups; the others were waiting in the wings to see what would happen. I knew that I would have to face the wing about it, but I felt confident in myself that the circumstances in which it occurred would be sufficient explanation. I appeared on the wing the following day along with the four others who had admitted smoking dope the night Grendon closed; the vote of the community in each case was 'to stay'. The staff group were to consider the cases the following Monday. Joe Chapman was not going to be there and had written a memo recording a vote 'to stay' and listing the work that had been done at Winchester.

At 3.30 on Monday afternoon, just three days after arriving at Wellingborough, I was called to see Roger Cruickshank, who informed me that the staff group had considered the case and the result was that I should leave. To say I was surprised would be an understatement, but I was particularly aggrieved because only three of the eleven staff group members who voted that day were Grendon staff; the rest were from Wellingborough and had never set eyes on me in their life! Later that day I asked one of them, Ben Steggles, why he had felt it necessary to vote me out of the community; his reply was to ask me for my name – which says it all. The real reasons only became apparent a few days later when Joe returned. He was angry that a vote had been taken and more so when he discovered that his memo and vote had not even been referred to or recorded; so much for democracy. It transpired that a small number of officers who were not in the least interested in Grendon – and who had all applied for transfers to other establishments – had used their influence to swing the vote.

The panto was now very much up and running again. Michael Selby, Grendon's governor – now in charge at Wellingborough – clearly wanted to use it as a public relations exercise for the locals who had been fed all kinds of rubbish by the Wellingborough POA. Russell took over the running of the panto because it was not clear whether I was going to be around long enough to see it performed. I did indeed leave before it was produced, but Joe Chapman wrote and told me that it had been a great evening and had raised several hundred pounds for local handicapped children.

Mike Lambe was as good as his word and bought the writing course for me. I threw myself into it and used it as a way of getting rid of excess energies. Though I was now in the process of being transferred out of Grendonborough I had opted to remain in therapy so that I could continue to obtain as much benefit as possible and attend group and community meetings.

I had many books to read and had just completed one by Judge James Pickles, *Straight From The Bench*. I was immediately struck by the style of his writing and his sense of humour; any circuit judge who can call a press conference in a pub and call his boss – the Lord Chancellor – 'an ancient dinosaur' has earned more than a modicum of my respect! I wrote and invited him to the social evening that was being planned, another of Mike Selby's propaganda efforts for the locals. I was surprised that he replied at all, but he did so, regretting that he was unable to attend but thanking me for my invitation. The matter was left at that; or so I thought.

I spoke to Joe Chapman a great deal during this period. I had come a long way in the year I had been a part of the Grendon regime and I was not about to throw it all away because a few staff had chosen to act like children. Life is unfair at times and this is not an ideal world. Tough. We have to make the best of what we have and carry on along the road avoiding, as far as possible, the potholes along the way. It was tempting to blame the staff group, and they did indeed have some blame to shoulder, but I was the one who had smoked the dope on the night that Grendon had closed and it was no use trying to blame everyone else but myself. The community had shown their displeasure at what had taken place by recording, for the first time in the history of Grendon, a vote of no confidence in the staff group; the transplantation of Grendon had not been without its problems.

Throughout the previous year I had been involved in a legal battle against the Home Office over the fourteen-year-old compulsory deduction of 3p per week from the wages of convicted prisoners; known as the common fund. I was doing an essay on the 1689 Bill of Rights when I came across the requirement that there could be 'no taxation without the authority of Parliament'; was the common fund a taxation and did they have Parliamentary approval for it? It was certainly deducted at source and compulsory and I could find no authority for this deduction in either the Prison Act or the Prison Rules. When I invited the Home Secretary to identify his statutory authority for the deduction, I was rewarded with a pregnant silence from the Home Office. When it became clear that they were fobbing me off I started proceedings for judicial review; two days before the case was due to come to court, the Home Office issued Circular Instruction 7/90 to all prison governors which abolished the levy forthwith. This was reported in a front-page article in the *Guardian* on 12 March 1990: 'Cell Lawyer opens way to £1m Claims'! The very same day the Home Office issued instructions that I was to be transferred to HM Prison Blundeston in Suffolk; *C'est la vérité qui blesse*, as the French would say!

Joe and I spent a few hours talking about this development. Transfers usually take at least three months to arrange and I had been moved on in just four weeks. I was very sad that I was leaving, but I would also remain very grateful for the opportunity Grendon gave me to change my life. Joe told me to keep in touch; 'You now have everything you need to make a success of your life.' I have kept in touch with him and have enjoyed doing so; even if – two years later – he has still not found time to send me the photos of the panto!

Grendon has many faults, but its benefits far outweigh them. The two largest problems, therapeutically speaking, are the Home Office policy which, first, insists on putting a disciplinary governor – and not a medical officer – in charge of the establishment, and, secondly, posts officers to Grendon who have no desire to be there and are a disruptive influence not only on the inmates but on the other staff as well. I was told one day, quite candidly, by an officer called Steve: 'I did not join the prison service to help prisoners with their problems, I have enough of my own. I've applied for a transfer to another establishment, and I've been waiting for eighteen months for it to come through; I just cannot seem to fit in with the regime here.' The Home Office are not doing anyone any favours by posting staff to Grendon who do not wish to be there; conversely I have met a number of staff stranded in the system who would like nothing better than to work at Grendon; swapping the two seems to be beyond Home Office ability. Prisoners are required to volunteer for Grendon, so why should staff be any different? They have a vital role to play within the therapeutic regime and it is crucial that they should all be willing; like prisoners, some are cut out for a place in a therapeutic regime and others are not.

Perhaps the most obvious problem with Grendon comes as a result of its poor image within the prison system. Despite being open for almost thirty years it remains the only therapeutic prison in the United Kingdom; France, by comparison, has built fourteen therapeutic prisons since 1976. Prisoners and prison officers in the penal system do not really know what Grendon does. They have a twisted impression brought about by a mixture of fact and fable, and that does not help anyone. If the Home Office really wishes to learn from the Grendon experience, the first thing they need to do is make sure that everyone knows what the place is about. A video showing Grendon in action has been mentioned but never put into practice, and that would be a start. Literature packs should be developed and dispersed, giving information on how to apply, who would be thought suitable and how to make the first step. Grendon is too valuable to be isolated.

I left Grendonborough with sadness. On the morning of my departure the lads came up to my cell to wish me farewell and I shook the hands of all of my group members. As I looked around the wing I found it hard to believe that I was taking this so easily; as little as a year before they would have had to wrap me in a body belt. I made my way to the reception, along with Eddie the Eagle who was making his third move in as many months, and climbed into the taxi waiting by the reception. As the large gates closed behind me and we headed towards Lowestoft I was determined that the lessons of the last twelve months would not be forgotten.

PART FOUR

Into the Home Straight

I arrived at Blundeston on 20 March 1990, three years and five months to the day since I was unceremoniously kicked out of it in 1986. Within a few days of being back in the system I became aware of the same tension in the prison as that I had experienced at Winchester the previous month.

Blundeston had already experienced a riot, two months before my arrival, which started in the dining hall after a senior officer allegedly attacked a prisoner with a truncheon. What-ever the truth of that incident, it resulted in a violent disturbance which Blundeston's governor, Josephine Fowler (also known affectionately as the Wicked Witch), had skilfully contained to one wing, and had brought to an end within forty-eight hours. The cause of this tension, which was not restricted to Blundeston but was present nationally, lay ultimately with the Home Office Prison Department who had been misleading prison staff since a 1987 industrial agreement restructured prison officers' working hours. Dissatisfaction by prison officers soon begins to affect prisoners and is a recipe for conflict and chaos.

The 'fresh start' working agreement of 1987 between the Home Office and the POA completely restructured working practices. In return for the abolition of overtime, which prison officers had abused for decades, the Home Office promised an improved basic wage, the recruitment of extra staff and the staged reduction to a thirty-nine-hour working week for all officers by April 1992. In November 1987, when 'fresh start' came into effect, prison officers were contracted for a maximum of forty-nine hours per week. This was to be reduced by two hours per year until, in April 1992, there was a unified thirty-nine-hour working week. The agreement stipulated that, save in exceptional and clearly defined circumstances, officers who were required to work in excess of their contracted hours would not be paid for them; they could, however, bank and convert those hours to 'Time Off In Lieu' (TOIL) – but only when the governor had enough staff on duty to permit it.

The practical problems of 'fresh start' only became apparent after it was implemented. Officers found themselves in an almost impossible position. It was inevitable that large amounts of TOIL would be earned because it was not possible to make a smooth transition to reduced hours without extra staff. But employing extra staff took time, and the government was building thirty *new* prisons which swallowed up far more than the new staff promised under 'fresh start'.

As the amounts of TOIL increased across the country and prison officers found they could not take their time off, working pressures increased and staff began to go sick with stress-related illnesses. This added to the workload placed on their colleagues. The shortage of staff that caused the TOIL to be earned in the first place was precisely the reason why it could not be taken. The POA constantly made media statements about 'manning levels' and the Home Office in turn rebutted their claims with disingenuous statements that all was well. Unable to take the TOIL they had earned, prison officers engaged in a work-to-rule. Staff across the country refused to work more than their contracted hours and, as the number of staff on duty fell, prison governors – who were caught between the Home Office demands of more prisoners to the pound and the POA claims that you can't run a penal system on a shoestring – responded in the only way possible: internal prison regimes were reduced and prisoners were locked in their cells. It came as no surprise when, on Sunday, 1 April 1990, Manchester's Strangeways prison erupted in a twenty million pound orgy of violence, destruction and death.

I had been allocated to an eight-man dormitory on D Wing of Blundeston, but within a week I had found myself a single cell on B Wing, whose tenancy I was to hold for the next year. Every night throughout April the television room was packed for the Six O'Clock News as the BBC catalogued the nationwide prison riots and collapse of the prison system. I spoke to many staff during this period and each of them pointed the finger of blame not at the prisoners occupying the rooftops, but at the faceless Whitehall authorities who made decisions affecting thousands of prisoners and staff but who had never worked within a prison; the then director-general of the Prison Service, Christopher Train (who took early retirement following the allegations of lack of leadership levelled at him after the riots) was a typical example.

Jimmy Boyle, perhaps Britain's most famous prisoner of recent times, was interviewed during the riots and passionately argued the case for reform. 'An increasing number of angry young men have taken to the roofs of our prisons and raised anguished voices in a guttural cry of despair – enough is enough. There is a need to listen to this alternative voice.' In London, Lord Justice of Appeal Sir Harry Woolf was listening and, within a week, had been appointed to head a public and judicial inquiry into the riots.

When Lord Justice Woolf was appointed, my immediate reaction was to fear a Home Office whitewash. Before he became a High Court judge in 1980 – from where he was subsequently promoted to the Court of Appeal – Harry Woolf had been the senior counsel of the Home Office Prison Department. He had earned himself a reputation as a formidable advocate and had been responsible for defeating many cases brought by prisoners. From my cell at Blundeston I decided to write to him. This inquiry was too important to have its report open to the criticism, before it even began, that the head of the inquiry had a vested interest in absolving his previous employers of blame. I had appeared before Lord Justice Woolf in the Court of Appeal in September 1986 when he granted leave to move for judicial review in the case which ultimately went to the House of Lords and as a judge I had great respect for him. I voiced my fears that the report of causes of prison riots and their dreadful human and physical costs was too important to be overshadowed by claims of partiality. He replied quite quickly saying that he had carefully considered all I had to say but he was capable of being impartial and he shared my views that it was important to get to the bottom of the matter. When his 600-page report into the riots was published it was praised by all interested parties as a magnificent document which, if acted upon, would take the English penal system firmly into the twenty-first century. I am happy to record my fears were quite groundless.

The riots of April 1990 provided me with a subject for my first newspaper article, which looked at the disciplinary system of the Board of Visitors; many prisoners then occupying our prison rooftops would subsequently make an appearance before them. Entitled 'Watchdogs on a Tightrope' it was published in the *Guardian* on 10 May. I had made my entrance as a journalist.

Many prisoners who saw me discussing prison issues with prison staff were suspicious and sometimes openly hostile. It was a time of great pressures for me. I often wanted to take a step back and so reinforce the divide which has traditionally separated staff from inmates (and resulted in much of the chaos in our penal system). Staff too are faced with this divide when they develop a professional relationship with their charges. I often talked to Prison Officer Stan Bensley, one of that small band of professional officers who sees his job as consisting of more than locking and unlocking doors; he goes out of his way to help prisoners who have problems, and earns the respect of inmates and the criticism of colleagues. There are few officers who recognise that no matter how much money is thrown at the penal system, reform will only come when attitudes on both sides change.

In June 1990 I returned briefly to Scotland to hear the case against the Scottish Secretary of State which I had started while at Inverness prison in 1987. Scottish prison rules – like their English counterparts which I was later similarly to challenge in London – insist that letters between a prisoner and his legal adviser only become 'privileged', and therefore free from censorship, when a writ has been issued. If a prisoner writes to his solicitor saying, 'I have been assaulted by Officer Smith', and wishes to bring proceedings against the officer, all letters passing between the prisoner and solicitor are subject to censorship – perhaps by Officer Smith himself – until a writ has been issued. Legal aid to issue a writ averages four months, and is dependent on first obtaining the written supporting advice of a barrister. This not only runs against the doctrine of legal privilege, it is also contrary to a judgement of the House of Lords (*Waugh v. BRB* [1979], 2 All ER 1169).

I persuaded Colin McEachran QC to support my case that this provision was unlawful and so in June we appeared before Lord Caplan in the Court of Session in Edinburgh. The Secretary of State was represented by Scotland's Solicitor-General, which gives a good indication of the seriousness with which the case was viewed. Ultimately we lost after Lord Caplan held it was not unlawful because a solicitor could always privately visit his client. On 25 March 1992 the European Court of Human Rights, in the case of *Campbell v. UK*, rejected that approach and held that solicitors' letters may not be read, whether proceedings have been issued or not. My case is now destined for the House of Lords.

On my way back to Blundeston in July, I had the misfortune to stop off for a week in HMP Durham. It is a filthy, vermin-infested prison, and the absence of any staff/inmate relationship makes it depressing and inhuman too. On the date I was due to return to Blundeston I was unlocked at 6 a.m. and taken to the prison reception. At 8.45 a.m. as the prison coach was about to depart, an officer discovered a page from my prison record had been left in the prison's administration office. Instead of waiting fifteen minutes until it opened, the officers returned me to my cell and sent the coach on its way. The result, as I wrote in the *Guardian* a week later, was that a taxi had to be ordered and two more officers used to take me to Blundeston; the cost to the taxpayer for the 600-mile round trip to Lowestoft was almost £1000.

At Blundeston I was reunited with Eddie the Eagle, whom I'd missed during my month away. He'd been cared for by another prisoner who was pleased to be rid of him; he had spent three days trying to get Eddie back in his cage after he'd 'escaped'. There was a load of mail awaiting my return. One letter was from Ned Chaillet, a BBC Radio 4 drama producer who was producing my play, 'The Facts Speak for Themselves'. He came to see me and we discussed the script. I had to rewrite two of the characters before he said he was satisfied. Another letter waiting for me was from a man called Andy Bell. When he visited I discovered he was a journalist with Granada TV's 'World in Action', researching a programme on body belts, strip cells and ghostings. He asked for my help; I readily agreed. This was not simply a desire to expose the penal system's barbaric methods of enforcing discipline, however. Since Grendon my views had altered. I was now more interested in showing the way forward than criticising for the sake of it.

Over the next six months I had a number of 'secret' meetings with Andy Bell. The prison had no idea he was from Granada TV and the Wicked Witch would have had kittens if she had found out! Andy was always very careful – and I've since learned from a number of sources that he's not beyond using an alias to get into prisons where his name is known. The meetings with Andy ended with a four-hour filming session and I was delighted with the result when 'The Ghostrain' was broadcast in April 1991; the governor's comment, 'Leech, words fail me', was said with a twinkle in the eye.

The *Guardian* began publishing my pieces each month and, while I often received letters as a result, I was simply inundated when 'Locked Into a Fight for Survival' was published on 17 October 1990 – I received 700 letters. I had been inspired to write after the September crime figures – breaking all previous records once again – were met with the police blaming the government for a lack of resources and the government blaming everyone from the courts to the victims themselves. I made the point that it is not the number of prison places that has to be addressed but the number of criminals. Building more prisons will no more reduce the crime rate than building more hospitals will reduce the number of road accidents. We have to create more Grendon Underwoods and fewer Dartmoors. It's not much use training a prisoner to be a bricklayer unless you train the bricklayer not to burgle houses, I reiterated.

Rochester, Kent
17 October 1990

Dear Mark,
Your article in today's *Guardian* was very thought-provoking and gave a good diagnosis of the problem. In particular the point about the burglar/ bricklayer and hospital/road accidents stick in the mind. The statistical evidence about the 15–21 age group is also interesting – unfortunately my younger son is an example but so far has just avoided prison . . .
PJB

Reading, Berks

Dear Mark Leech,
I hope you will forgive this intrusion on your privacy, but I so wanted to write to offer you

my sincere support for what you are doing and what you have already achieved ... men of your determination deserve so much.

VJM

Halifax, W. Yorks

Dear Mark,

So far I agree with everything you have written. I hope that jointly we may make a real contribution to penal reform.

(Judge) James Pickles

London SW1

Dear Mark Leech,

I wonder if you will receive lots of mail in response to your article 'Locked into a Fight for Survival' in today's *Guardian*. I was very impressed because you have reiterated what I have been convinced about and arguing for, for years. But you speak with the voice of experience and therefore authority. It occurs to me that seeing my address and nice notepaper you may well have very mixed feelings about this letter. I'm middle-class, middle-aged and middle-income (that sounds like the type of 'do-gooder' which even I despise) but however different we may be we share certain beliefs as your article demonstrated; thank you for it.

GMcM

As Christmas 1990 approached and I finally came within sight of the all-important home-leave threshold of nine months from release, I applied for a three-day leave for the weekend 8–11 February, and was delighted when it was granted. Pat and Arthur were visiting when they could and my dad came regularly from his home in Birmingham to see me. He was delighted with the way things were going and apparently had copies of all of my articles on his wall!

In January 1991 I read of a young offender who had committed suicide while in a punishment block strip cell. That incident inspired me to write 'Blinded by Prejudice', my first attempt at writing a 90-minute play for television. Judge James Pickles wrote to me with a whole list of questions on prisons, and also to say he had decided to retire in July 1991 and was currently writing his second book. I was pleased to give him all the help I could; and so began a correspondence and a friendship that exists to this day. It was thanks to Jim Pickles that I came to meet my literary agent, and it was Jim Pickles who first suggested that I write this book.

After 'Blinded by Prejudice' I turned back to writing radio plays and wrote 'Without Fear or Favour' (a 60-minute radio play about a rebellious circuit judge) during the course of five days when I had to be dragged away from my typewriter to eat or slop out. My writing was occupying my every waking minute. I submitted both plays to the 1991 Koestler Awards and also sent a copy of each to my agent, who passed them to his drama agent. Both plays came back to me with a brief note saying my agent had been advised they were not highly thought of. Much later in the year 'Blinded by Prejudice' won the Koestler First Prize for Playwriting for Television – and also won the BBC Script Unit Award 1991. 'Without Fear or Favour' won the John Mortimer First Prize for Playwriting for Radio.

On 8 February 1991 I woke early and was ready to go on home leave – with Eddie the Eagle who was to be left with Pat – long before the electronic lock on my cell door sprung itself and released me. I had quite a lot of luggage in addition to the budgie and, rather than drag it all across the London Underground, decided instead to hire a car and drive to Bristol; repeating the journey I had made in October 1986. Perhaps I should have learned my lesson from that journey: three miles outside Lowestoft the heavens opened and the whole of southern England came to a standstill in blizzard conditions. I eventually arrived home in Bristol eleven hours later.

The weekend was filled with meetings. In addition to 'bumping into a camera crew from World in Action' – as I later explained it to the governor – I had meetings with my agent and publisher and spent a blissfully happy afternoon with my dad in Birmingham. I spent most of my 'spare' time with a close friend who, for reasons which will become apparent, I shall not call by his real name, but by the name David. On Monday, when I was due to return to Blundeston, the weather in Bristol was fine but freezing. I desperately didn't want to go back; my first taste of freedom in four long years had been intoxicating and as the crucial time for departure arrived, I faltered. Fortunately Pat was there and would have none of the I'll-see-the-doctor-and-say-I've-hurt-my-back routine – thankfully. I left Bristol and headed out east along the M4; the further east I went the worse the conditions became and I found myself in snow every bit as bad as the previous Friday. The A12 was first blocked for three hours and then closed completely. Accidents littered the roads and at each one I asked the police, involved in clearing the road, to endorse my parole licence with name and telephone number – foresight is better than being wise after the event. I eventually arrived back at Blundeston at 2 a.m., eleven hours late, exhausted but in one piece. I was welcomed back with open arms; unfortunately they belonged to a prison officer who handed me a 'telegram' for being late! I was given a caution by the governor after I protested that if they imposed so much as one minute of punishment, they'd have to justify it in front of the High Court!

Soon after my return to Blundeston I was given a security 'D' classification – suitable for open prison conditions – and within a few weeks was informed I was being transferred to Leyhill open prison, a mile from junction 14 of the M5 in Gloucestershire. I left Blundeston for Leyhill on 28 March 1991, one year, one week and one day after I had arrived there.

Leyhill open prison started out as a wartime American army base but since 1986 has been completely rebuilt. Judge Stephen Tumim, HM Chief Inspector of Prisons, described Leyhill as the 'Jewel in the Prison Service crown', but in my view it does not deserve that accolade and, in many ways, was far more petty and restrictive than the maximum-security prisons I have been to. Open prisons are a contradiction in terms. I have often been puzzled by the philosophy that sends a man to prison because a non-custodial sentence is inappropriate, but then decides conversely that he represents no risk to the public. You can't have it both ways. If a man is not a danger to the public then there are many other non-custodial sentencing options, less expensive but equally punitive.

I found the transition from closed to wholly open conditions very difficult to make. I was allocated to B Unit, one of two residential units, each holding 200 prisoners. Leyhill promotes itself as a place that gives prisoners every opportunity to make a success of release. In reality it is little more than a cheap labour camp for the rest of the penal system; churning out peeled potatoes by the truckload and printing stationery for a Home Office that has not yet understood the meaning of conservation. The prison has won awards from the Royal Horticultural Society for its gardens, and camera crews are pushed in so frequently by the Home Office press department that prisoners should qualify for an Equity card. It is all stage-managed, from the tractor driving past with the smiling inmate at the wheel, to the goldfish swimming serenely in the pool outside the governor's office.

Leyhill does have some good points, but it would have many more if the Home Office would reappraise its function, perhaps turn it into a huge pre-release hostel helping its prisoners – many of whom are at the end of long sentences – to reintegrate into society. From the governor, the splendidly named Nick Wall, to the most junior member of staff, the frustration at not being able to do more is keenly felt. The governor comes in for some unfair criticism. I know, I've done it myself; succumbing to the easy temptation of blaming him for what is the fault of Home Office officials who simply do not know what they are doing.

I had been at Leyhill a month when fate intervened once more and put in train a series of events I could never have foreseen. I'd come a long way in four years and the future looked good: I was still writing pieces regularly for the *Guardian* as well as other periodicals, I'd written three plays and was hard at work on a fourth, this book was almost done and release was just six months away. I think it's called sod's law. I got a letter from David in Cardiff, whom I had last seen during my home leave three months before.

> Dear Mark,
>
> This is going to be a very difficult letter to write. I've agonised over it for 2 weeks but I have to tell you that a recent HIV test which I had was positive. I don't know how else to tell you this, but it's important that you have the test too. I had no idea in February I can assure you, it's come as a great shock. Do write and let me know you're OK . . .

I sat there and read and reread the letter. Letters at Leyhill are not censored so the prison authorities did not know what the letter had said. The abrupt change in my behaviour must have signalled something was wrong. Over the next few weeks my relationship with everyone around me deteriorated, then disintegrated. I became angry and abusive, and found myself on three disciplinary reports in as many days – my first in three years with the exception of returning late to Blundeston. I went from high to low, from warm to cold and from serene to red-hot angry and back again. All my time at Grendon should have taught me to discuss it with someone, anyone, but I was unable to do so. Sometimes I thought I was worrying over nothing. I got close a number of times to speaking about it to my wing principal officer, Dave Little, who was clearly perplexed by my behaviour. The governor was running out of patience with me. He held monthly inmate meetings where he invited the whole prison to meet the local management team and raise important issues. I stood in front of 400 prisoners and castigated him for his inability to run the prison, shouting from the back of the visiting room, blaming him for what was my own inability to deal with the problem that was destroying me.

I finally did have the test done during a day parole. The test at the Genito-Urinary Clinic was preceded by a brief chat as to my reaction were the result to be positive. My reply still rings in my ears: 'I had flu a few weeks ago and got over that OK, this is just a precaution.' I was told to return a week later for the results. I was commissioned by the *Guardian* to travel to the Halifax home of Judge Pickles in mid-June to interview him before his retirement on 1 July, and I collected the test results on my way back to Leyhill. It took me twenty minutes to pluck up the courage to go in and collect them – and I spent the next three hours sitting in the car park, cursing every God I knew – and half a dozen I didn't – but the verdict of HIV positive remained the same; I was poleaxed.

I arrived back at Leyhill four hours late and not in the best of moods. The terse two-word welcome from the irate principal officer on the gate, 'You're nicked', was met with an equally terse two-word reply which did nothing to help the situation. I spent the next forty-eight hours in a state of bewilderment, unable to discuss it with anyone as I oscillated between the deranged certainty that the results were wrong and the rational knowledge that they were correct. Unfinished articles and unanswered letters littered my table and the Pickles interview I had spent four months researching was pushed out of sight; my future had suddenly become totally meaningless. I tried to visualise the unwanted and invading virus running through my veins, wondering what it looked like, where it had come from. *Why* was there no cure? All these thoughts rushed through my brain and, as I stared at the ceiling of my cell, only added to the utter and devastating confusion which raged within me.

Dave Little came into the wing office as I was waiting to collect my mail two days after I received the results. We found ourselves alone as staff went out to deal with a visiting probation officer. He looked at me and said, quite calmly, 'Mark, what is wrong with you?' I tried to speak but my lips trembled and tears began to flow down my cheeks. I could not get the words out. That evening I flipped into self-destruct when I absconded from Leyhill open prison in an effort to leave behind me a world which had once again become too complex to handle.

Fortunately money was not a problem. I'd recently collected more than a thousand pounds and I picked up my car and drove to Cardiff. I spoke to David and later in the evening we went out with friends to a pub. When I came out I found my car had been stolen. It was a long night, just sitting with friends trying to make sense out of my world which had been turned upside down; Four weeks ago I had a bright future, I was almost at the end of my sentence. Now I had no future and was on the run – without even a car to carry me away.

The following morning I hired a car and drove north to Scotland. I didn't understand about HIV and Aids. I was convinced I already had one foot in the grave and the other was soon to follow. What is HIV? I knew that the antibodies in my blood were evidence that I had come into contact with the virus that causes Aids, but what is a virus? How does it lead to Aids – what is Aids? As I drove up the motorway questions raged through my brain.

I stayed for a week with a friend, Maureen, in Ardrossan, an Ayrshire coastal town some forty miles west of Glasgow. Maureen had no idea I was on the run. I reasoned it was better that she didn't know as that way she could not be accused of 'harbouring'; she would not have asked me to leave and not telling her was a way of protecting her. She thought I had recently been released and had come north to get away from pressures down south. I had known 'Mo' about five years and stayed with her before – she knew I was gay and completely accepted it.

A mile from Mo's lived another friend of mine – whom I shall call Peter. He invited me to visit him and his wife, Margaret. We arranged that I would come the following Saturday, 29 June, and stay overnight; I intended to return to England on Sunday and go back to Cardiff where I had learned my car was sitting in the police compound after being in collision with a taxi. The car I had hired in Cardiff was now overdue and the police would be looking for it. I had hired the car on my own licence and knew I would eventually be caught. I didn't even want to think about going back to prison. My mind was in turmoil. I could not think straight; lost in the depths of my hopeless predicament I was simply writing myself off, and set against that an overdue hire car paled into insignificance.

I arrived at Peter's about 1 p.m. the following Saturday, having said goodbye to Mo and thanked her for letting me stay. I had met Peter while working in the kitchen of Perth prison in 1987, where he had been serving an eight-year sentence for robbery. His wife Margaret was a witty Glaswegian who had me in stitches, a diversion from the things occupying my thoughts for which I was grateful. Peter, like Mo, did not know I was on the run, nor was he aware of my sexuality since he knew me from a time when I was still firmly locked in the proverbial closet. His sister Laura was visiting when I arrived and it was clear Peter was working towards pairing us off . . . Peter asked about the car and I told him it was stolen – as it was by then – from Cardiff; not adding I had hired it on my own licence. The four of us went to Kilmarnock in the afternoon and spent the time window-shopping and having a drink in a city-centre pub. Laura lived in Greenock and Peter, acting from admirable though misinformed intentions, asked if I would drive her home; I agreed. We arrived back in Ardrossan and as we were all hungry Peter suggested we pull in to a local café from where Peter and Margaret would walk the mile to their home while I drove Laura to Greenock; the Little Chef café we went into was to play a part in my life that I have still to recover from.

Laura and I arrived at her home in Greenock between 8 and 9 p.m. and as she was getting her handbag and coat from the back seat she announced she'd left her tablets at the Little Chef; I didn't even know she was taking any. Apparently Laura was epileptic and had taken a tablet in the café, leaving her bottle by mistake. I said I would call in on my way back, and she said she would phone them and ask the staff to put them to one side. She gave me her phone number and I left. When I arrived at the Little Chef the staff were preparing to go home. The manager had not found any tablets.

Back at Peter's I was told Laura had phoned to say she had found her tablets. I told Peter that I had called into the Little Chef and I explained what had taken place, stupidly repeating a comment made by the manager about their having taken £1800 that day. I went to bed and was soon asleep. The next day, Sunday, 30 June, I lay in bed until midday, when I could hear Peter and Margaret moving about downstairs. I was planning to leave that day, though for me there were no real 'plans' at all, I was living each day as it came along. Margaret was telling me about the karaoke night she had been to the previous Sunday at a local pub and by all accounts it sounded hilarious. She suggested I should stay and go and have a look; it took place every Sunday. A mixture of not really having anywhere to go in England and the inability at that time to make any real decisions, led to my agreeing. The Reaper pub sits just across from the estate and Peter asked if he could use the car while I was gone; 'I won't get caught, I know the area.' I gave him the spare set of keys and at 8.30 p.m. I set off for the Reaper and my first ever karaoke night.

Inside the pub, which had a small dance floor and a general seating area, I walked to the bar and ordered a drink. Two men were setting up electrical equipment and at 9 p.m. the karaoke began; the pub was quite full, and soon became packed to capacity. To my left at the bar stood a man who was in his mid-twenties and was clearly known to the two men who put on the karaoke night. We got talking. He told me he lived locally with his wife and had been due to go to Amsterdam the following Wednesday, but had had to cancel the trip because of a shortage of cash. I told him I had been to Amsterdam and so began a conversation which lasted most of the night. I left the Reaper after a great evening at 11 p.m. when the karaoke ended.

I noticed the car was not back, and I found Peter and two of his friends sitting in the lounge busily counting money; they had robbed the Little Chef and the police had subsequently discovered the car and hauled it away. I was furious. I was stranded in Scotland; they had not changed the plates on the car and the police would soon discover I'd hired it. Then it would be a simple matter of the police showing the people in the Little Chef my photo, with the inevitable result: 'He was in here last night.' I was not impressed to hear they had used iron bars instead of guns and the fact that they wore masks was cold comfort to me; it would have been better, from my point of view, if they'd shown their faces. I refused their offer of a share of the proceeds and the fact that I could 'hire a car in the morning' did nothing to lessen my anxiety. I told them exactly where I stood: I was on the run, the car had been hired on my own licence and I had been to the Little Chef twice yesterday – the manager would undoubtedly remember me and his own comment (unsolicited though it was) as to the takings. Not only that, both of the 'friends' were English and naturally had English accents. They assured me they had not spoken but I couldn't believe them. As the night wore on I gradually cooled down and tried to reason it through. I had to trace the man I spoke to in the Reaper, he alone could establish my alibi; but I only knew him as Billy. The two friends left at 3 a.m. and I fell asleep in the chair – 'sleep' is not the word to describe the nightmare I was experiencing.

On Monday I hired another car. I knew there was no prospect of me returning it but I had to get away from Scotland; I was running away again. By 4 p.m. I had left Scotland. I had less than £100 in cash, very few clothes and nowhere to run to; time was fast running out.

Everything I'd learned at Grendon, all the advice I'd been given, listened to and acted on in the past, deserted me. I was operating now on survival instincts, falling back on those criminal tendencies which had formed such an integral part of my life for so long – and which I had worked so hard to abandon. Feelings of total failure washed over me, and I hated myself. I knew deep down inside the only way forward was to confront the mess I was in, face it head on and start on the long road back. That night, in a hotel in Manchester, I phoned Leyhill prison and spoke to a startled Dave Little, my one-time unit principal officer. To his eternal credit he never pressured me to reveal where I was and promised that if I came back now there would be no heavy scene: 'We'll take you to reception, put the cuffs on and take you to Bristol prison.' How I wish I had had the courage to see it through; again I failed.

On Friday, 19 July, I was staying in a guest house in the Shirley district of Southampton. At 7 p.m. there was a knock on my room door and I opened it to be faced with half a dozen police officers. 'Mark Leech?' asked Detective Constable Philip Barbergallo. I nodded and six bewildering weeks of running and living off stolen credit cards had finally come to an end.

I was arrested and taken to Southampton's civic centre police station. As the cell door slammed shut behind me I lay down on the wooden bench, my mind in turmoil. Life has a strange habit of throwing up coincidences, as I have discovered more than once. In the corner of the cell was a newspaper and to pass the time I picked it up. Dated 6 July – my dad's birthday – this fortnight-old copy of the *Sun* contained the debut column of the newly retired Judge James Pickles; across the top of the page ran the headline 'Go back to jail, Mark'. He had written an impassioned piece, a plea for which I felt immense gratitude on one hand and absolute regret for its necessity on the other; it all seemed to belong to a lifetime away in the past.

The following day I found myself at Winchester prison. The memories of Grendon-in-Winchester came flooding back, my heart ached to turn back the clock. As I stood on the landing an officer came along: 'Well, if it isn't the chairman.' He laughed as he closed the door. 'I knew it was all bullshit.' He was wrong, and in that instant I started the long fight back.

I was not placed on report for absconding, they delayed too long to serve me with the 'telegram' and I was fortunate that the Winchester administration was as chaotic as ever. I knew the first thing I had to do was see the doctor and get some help. My head was up my arse (to use a prison saying). I was in turmoil about HIV and I needed to talk to someone. It proved harder than I imagined. The uniformed 'hospital' officer refused to let me see the doctor unless I told him of the problem; not an easy thing to shout through a piece of perspex when there are twenty prisoners in a line behind you!

I discovered there were leaflets on Aids and HIV published by the Prison Department, but instead of being given to prisoners on their reception into prison, they are left gathering dust in the wing office where a request to have one is immediately construed as an admission of guilt; there is also a video on Aids which, according to the Home Office, 'any prisoner can ask to see'. The Prison Department will tell you they have spent thousands training selected officers as Aids/HIV counsellors, but you will not find their names published on notice boards (HMP Bristol excepted); like the leaflets and the video, prisoners have to ask their landing officer – which is the same as writing it on a bed sheet and draping it across a prison rooftop.

There is a tremendous amount of ignorance and prejudice

attached to Aids/HIV in prisons, just as in society in general. The POA have campaigned for HIV-positive prisoners to be isolated – a backward step typical of their traditional approach to penal policies in general and their ignorance of the subject in particular. If ever the Prison Department returns to an isolationist policy all they will achieve is the silence of HIV-positive prisoners and the ultimate price of the continued spread of the virus.

I had to re-establish contact with Pat and Arthur. They had not heard from me for two months and were, I later found, frantic with worry. They had kept track of my movements via the police who kept calling about the hire cars. What could I tell them? I could not tell them about the HIV because it would have been all round the jail by lunchtime. Instead I told them I had been under a great deal of pressure – true, but not wholly informative. Their reply was cautious and I knew they had been deeply hurt. My dad, too, was upset but held his own counsel.

In August I was moved to Shepton Mallet where I started sessions with a visiting HIV counsellor, Tony Hewitt from the Bristol Drugs Project. He listened as I poured out my fears and the way the news had affected me. Sex had held absolutely no attraction for me from the day I heard the news; a common reaction I now know.

DC Philip Barbergallo came to see me and asked me questions about the use of a stolen credit card, with which I had bought clothes and food for some two weeks. I had already decided that there would be no ducking the issue. I would admit exactly what I had done and pay the price for it. My decision to take that approach was reinforced by the attitude – refreshingly different I might add – of Philip Barbergallo. He was keen of course to do his job as a police officer, but there was also a human side which does not accord with the generally held perception of the police. He wanted to know why I had taken my 'eye off the ball and driven into the bunker' when everything at Leyhill seemed so promising.

Strathclyde police first made contact with the governor of Winchester prison, I later found out, a month after my re-arrest. They told the governor that they intended to charge me with robbery and though I knew I was innocent, I also felt the police would be so convinced of my guilt that little would persuade them otherwise. I subsequently wrote to Charles Knox, a well respected criminal trial lawyer from Glasgow, and got him to act for me.

I applied to the governor in late September for a three-day parole leave in early October to attend civil proceedings at the High Court. It was clear that Governor Beetlestone was conscious of my previous absconding but I gave him my word that I would return (I had nothing to fear from Scotland either) and he granted it. On 1 October I walked out of Shepton Mallet to be met by Pat – sheer heaven! I'd told her on the phone (finally!) about the HIV result and I was grateful that she didn't ask too many probing questions. The following day I won an order for the reinstitution of pro-ceedings against the Home Office at the High Court and all too quickly the time came to go back. I had no real difficulty. I was due out again the following week for a seven-day leave and as Pat dropped me off at the gate we took comfort from the fact that we'd be together again soon.

The day before I was due to go on my week's home leave I heard Strathclyde police had obtained an arrest warrant charging me with robbery. I decided not to tell Pat and Arthur or my dad because it would have soured the atmo-sphere and we could do without that. The week of leave sped by like an Intercity 125. I had a lovely afternoon with my dad but the difficult task of telling him about the HIV result. I had dreaded doing so, but it had to be done. I had taken advice on how to do it. We went for a drink in a local pub and it was a beautiful afternoon. Dad took the news remarkably well.

Arriving back at Shepton Mallet it was hard to walk through the gate with what I knew lay ahead. But I had learned my lesson and was not going to make the mistake of running away again.

The day after my return I received notification from the governor that he was returning to me the eleven days remission I had lost during the last four and a half years; the reasons he wrote as follows:

No loss of remission since 1 April 1989. Last report Leyhill 25 May 1991. Has responded to trust placed in him on home leave and temporary release. Conduct is generally 'good'. Constructive attitude, and uses his time to advantage at work.

The effect of this was to bring my date of release forward from 9 December 1991 to 28 November 1991; perhaps an academic result, given the determination of Strathclyde police to arrest me on release. They had still not been to interview me, as one would have expected – there are, after all, two sides to every story, though not apparently in Scottish legal procedure! As events developed, however, they were not prepared to wait for my release.

Four days after my return from leave I received a second memo from the governor:

CF1449 Leech M.

I have to inform you that I expect to receive an order for transfer for trial (Criminal Justice Act 1961 – section 28(i)) authorising me to transfer you to Scotland (HM Prison Edinburgh) for the purpose of your attendance at criminal proceedings. Such transfer is expected to take place on October 23rd 1991 via the National Escort System.

JRS Shergold
Governor
HM Prison Shepton Mallet
October 18th 1991

On 23 October, I was transferred to Durham and, the following morning, to HMP Edinburgh. Three days later I was moved to Glasgow's Barlinnie prison – one of the most brutal and inhuman penal establishments I've ever been in. Nestling beside the busy M8, some three miles from Glasgow's city centre, Barlinnie has an awesome reputation which is as well deserved as it is well known. Its five main residential halls hold some 900 prisoners in conditions which make England's Brixton and Wandsworth prisons seem almost Hilton-like.

I was placed in the convicted E Hall as my sentence was not yet finished. Here the atmosphere was tense, doors banged all day long, officers screamed and shouted and both sides were so far apart that they each – staff and prisoners alike – withdrew to the perceived safety of their own kind and never made any attempt to reach out to each other's side and solve what are common problems.

The prison clothing, red and white striped shirt and woollen baggy trousers made from army-type blanket material, did nothing to instil any degree of self-respect. Clothing was changed once a week, with each prisoner being allowed one shirt and one pair of socks and underpants (often in an appalling state) which had to last the whole week. Staff wore a police-style uniform, with slashed peaks on their caps, worn so the peak fell down and rested on the bridge of the nose; something condemned by Lord Justice Woolf as intimidating and not to be tolerated.

Basic facilities were lacking. Washing bowls were not issued and those circulating in the hall were passed from prisoner to prisoner on discharge – or could be bought when tobacco was short for a quarter ounce of Old Holborn. Chamber pots were at a premium and I made do with an old detergent bottle; shaving brushes are highly prized, as are pillows and extra blankets. Food was frequently cold and always unappetising – no matter how cold the weather, the Scottish prison system insists that once per week the tea meal will consist of one slice of cheese and one spoon of jam. Cells are in a disgusting state, paint flaking off ceilings and food and graffiti competing for space on the walls. I wrote a letter to the governor of Barlinnie, Englishman Peter Withers. I never received the promised written reply. To be fair he has inherited an appalling problem not of his own making and staff tend to be so militant that every single piece of reform has to surmount an obstacle course of negotiation with the SPOA, the Scottish Prison Officers' Association.

I was put in a workshop called 14 Party. It belongs to another century and is both humiliating and worthless. There is no work in 14 Party, the day (8.15–11.30 and 1.15–3.45) consists of sitting with forty or so other prisoners on hard chairs, totally idle, or walking (*Midnight Express* style) in an aimless shuffle around a small concrete square.

When Charles Knox came to visit we discussed the case and I found myself facing a straightforward man; he listed the problems. There were no witnesses to my alibi that I had been in the Reaper public house and, if my account of events was correct, it was a simple matter of impeaching those who carried out the robbery. But no one likes a 'grass' and those who went into the Little Chef, masked and carrying iron bars, could ensure I paid a terrible price for my revelations. In the real world a case does not end with the verdict. There is also another point to remember, for it is easy to become side-tracked by the 'should I name them or not' argument; I am not charged with withholding evidence as to the identity of the real culprits; I am charged with committing a robbery, and I did not do that.

On 31 October I was taken to Kilmarnock police station, which is attached to the court building. The charges were read over to me and on the advice of my lawyer I made no reply to the two policemen, who were not involved in the case but were simply there to charge me. In eighteen seconds I was remanded in custody for a week. There were three charges: theft of a hire car from Cardiff, robbery 'with persons unknown' of the Little Chef and theft of a hire car from Kilmarnock on the day after the robbery. Scottish law does not – unlike that in England – permit a bail application while a sentence is being served. I would therefore have to apply for bail on 28 November when my sentence expired. The police had still not sought to interview me and the procurator fiscal – an allegedly impartial public prosecutor loosely analogous to the English crown prosecution service – did not exercise his right to judicially examine me; as far as the crown was concerned the verdict was in the bag and they had better things to do.

I attended, that afternoon, an identity parade at Kilmarnock police station. Of the six others on the line-up only one had ginger hair – he was much taller than me – and two of them had no hair at all! We raised and recorded objections and the parade went ahead. I could not see any of the fourteen people who passed through on the other side of the one-way glass but I suspect they consisted of police (who had chased me), Little Chef staff who had been robbed and those present the previous night when I had enquired about Laura's tablets. Ten of them picked me out, three 'weren't sure' and one was 'certain' it was someone else. Of the three people actually robbed on the night, two had been forced to lie face down on the floor. One of those two picked me out, while the other could not identify anyone. The third person, who had faced the robbers and handed over the cash, was certain it was someone else in the line-up.

Attempts were being made to identify Billy and my lawyer, thanks to Pat, had large photographs of me. I was pinning my hopes on the bail application. Time was precious because I desperately wanted to spend Christmas at home. The fiscal was objecting to bail on the grounds of 'previous convictions', 'the serious nature of the charge' and the fact that I had 'absconded from Leyhill'.

On 28 November, four days before bail was refused, I had been taken from E Hall and, via the prison reception where I obtained a blue (untried) shirt for my red (convicted) one, was placed in C Hall which holds 250 untried prisoners in conditions far worse than in the rest of the prison.

In 1988 the Scottish penal system was hit by a series of riots every bit as violent and destructive as those that were to hit the English system two years later. Barlinnie suffered a ferocious riot in the prison's B Hall and the then governor implemented a lock-down system throughout the jail. 'Controlled unlocking' (or lock-down) confines all prisoners to their cells for twenty-three hours a day, no more than half a dozen being allowed out at any one time. It is strictly a short-term measure. Three and a half years after its introduction at Barlinnie, only the prison's C Hall is still subject to it; but there it has become accepted as the norm.

Breakfast is brought to the cell door at 7.30, dinner is served the same way at 10.30 and by 4 p.m. the tea meal has been consumed and the plate put outside the door. The next meal is up to eighteen hours away. Exercise consists of shuffling around a landing and I discovered that the regime also abolishes exercise completely every third weekend for an entire landing. On two out of three weekends, exercise is only given on a Saturday or a Sunday, but not both. Not only is that unforgivable when attached to a regime which employs twenty-three-hour lock-down, it is also directly contrary to prison (Scotland) rules and thus unlawful.

I appealed the refusal of bail to the Edinburgh High Court and told my lawyer that I wanted to present the application myself, to which he agreed. Locked in my cell my case occupied all of my waking hours. I had learned from others who had been 'fitted up' that it is a case of never giving up; it made me angry and that is what prevented me from collapsing in on myself.

I spent hours every day going through the case and my appeal against the refusal of bail. I had come too far along this road of change to give up and, though I had slipped and stumbled, I had picked myself up and was again moving forward. The sun finally broke through with the news that we had identified 'Billy' – William Thompson – and also had an address for him! I punched the air at the news.

On 8 December I was taken to the High Court for my bail appeal and I prayed it would be successful. The arguments appeared sound, but it was not to be. I was called into a small room to be faced by a judge who was already with the deputy fiscal who opposed the appeal; I have no way of knowing whether any discussions had already taken place, but it did not look good. I intended to argue that my previous convictions had to be balanced against my current achievements, but that was ruled 'irrelevant', and I was asked to go on to the next point. I tried to argue that I had successfully completed two home leaves and presented evidence from the governor of Shepton Mallet – it was brushed aside with contempt. 'You have five minutes,' the judge told me and at that point I realised it was hopeless; there is none so deaf as he who will not listen. I was taken back to Barlinnie within the hour and locked once more in my cell.

I found the lack of weekend exercise in C Hall difficult to accept. When you are locked up in a cell for twenty-three hours a day, that one hour outside of it becomes precious and a welcome relief. I was visited one morning in my cell by Barlinnie's governor, Peter Withers, and raised with him the abolition of exercise – pointing out that he had a clear statutory duty, under prison (Scotland) rules to provide it. He told me to go on a formal application and raise it through the 'proper channels'. I did so the next day and was seen by the hall governor, David Burnett. He accepted that under the rules exercise had to be provided, but explained he had a shortage of exercise yards; he told me he would arrange exercise when he had sorted out an exercise yard. The fact that this 'shortage of exercise yards' had remained unredressed for three and a half years and could in any event be corrected, in the interim, by using any one of the prison landings, tends to show that the local management at Barlinnie had little desire to resolve the matter.

Later in the day, while emptying my detergent bottle-cum-chamber pot, I mentioned to a fellow prisoner that weekend exercise was going to be reintroduced. This was overheard by a prison officer who asked me to repeat it, which I did, explaining what the hall governor had told me. Twenty minutes later the governor saw me and told me I had misunderstood him. Exercise was not being reintroduced straight away, but when he had found an exercise yard; the whole thing seemed to be a matter of semantics. I was placed on report for 'stating a falsehood' and found myself in solitary for the Good Order and Discipline of the prison. There is fierce resistance to any relaxation or alteration of the oppressive C Hall regime and I had paid the price for challenging it. By placing me in the segregation unit the authorities had killed two birds with one unjust stone: I got the weekend exercise I complained about, and the challenge to the C Hall regime was, at least for the moment, removed.

It is often said that a redeeming feature of the Scottish legal system is the rule, contained in the Criminal Procedure (Scotland) Act 1975, that a person can not be remanded in custody awaiting trial for longer than 110 days. However, not only is that subject to various legal exceptions, it also works against the defence in serious cases because of the system within which it operates. The 110-day period starts to run from the date of full committal for trial, which is normally a period of seven days after the first appearance. But unlike English procedural law, the Crown in Scotland do not release to the Defence any witness statements in their possession, nor are they required to satisfy the court that they have a prima facie case; committal for trial goes through 'on the nod', in less than twenty seconds. Defence must then set about discovering what the Crown's case is before they can even think of answering it.

For the first seventy-nine days after my committal I was given no details of the case against me. On the eightieth day I was served with an indictment which listed the charges against me and gave the names and addresses of some forty-one witnesses the Crown would call – but I was not entitled, even then, to be supplied with any details of what those witnesses would say. During the next thirty days my lawyer Charles Knox, who worked tirelessly on the case, had to track down all the Crown witnesses and ask them for a statement of their evidence, known in Scottish law as a 'precognition'. If witnesses are unwilling to provide a precognition, they cannot be compelled to do so. It then becomes a matter of hoping that they will tell you everything they have told the police. I was warned not to place too much reliance on the precognitions; if a witness in court alters their evidence from what they stated in their precognition, then Scottish law does not allow you to draw that to the attention of the jury. The precognition cannot be produced, nor the person who wrote it down called forward to give evidence – a rule typical of the system as a whole.

As the precognitions began to arrive, I obtained for the first time some idea of the Crown's case against me. The police had recovered from a local garden the batons, stocking masks and empty cash bags which, judging from the Little Chef cheques found in one of them, were clearly connected with the robbery. The police, not surprisingly, had been unable to link any of those items with me. Despite having a million-pound forensic laboratory in Glasgow, staffed by highly skilled scientists, and with nine months in which to achieve it, they had not been able to produce one single fingerprint, fibre of clothing or strand of hair which they could say, however loosely, was mine. Our greatest enemy was time; the 110-day clock was ticking away and, by the time it expired, we had still not obtained precognitions from ten of the Crown witnesses; we were in no position to go to trial.

Charles Knox and my barrister, Ronald Bain, sought a meeting with the prosecution and explained we could not proceed. The prosecution were not willing initially to agree to an adjournment, offering a week at the most. Ronald Bain, a formidable advocate who spent fifteen years as a Glasgow solicitor before going to the bar, made it clear he would have to withdraw from the case if they insisted on going to trial and, grudgingly, a sixty-day adjournment was agreed. I am currently lodging an application with the European Court of Human Rights, arguing that Scottish criminal procedure breaches Article Three of the European Convention on Human Rights; this guarantees that 'everyone charged with a criminal offence' has the right to 'be informed promptly, in a language which he understands and in detail, of the nature and cause of the accusation against him'. In my view, a delay of seventy-nine days after committal is not 'promptly' and the absence of witness statements does not inform me 'in detail' of 'the nature and cause of the accusation' against me.

The trial is now set for 13 April 1992 at the Kilmarnock High Court. As I write we are making progress in the preparation of the defence.

Perhaps the one commendable feature of Scottish law is the fact that a jury has three verdicts at its disposal: guilty, not proven and not guilty. The Crown have to prove their case beyond all reasonable doubt. I suspect there have been many cases in England where the jury have convicted where, had there been the option of a 'not proven' verdict, they would not have done so. Juries can often confuse a prima facie case, and the suspicion that that necessarily generates, with guilt beyond reasonable doubt. England would do well to adopt this aspect of the Scottish system, and I have written to the Royal Commission currently studying the criminal justice system to commend it to them.

As I lie on my bed, in the quiet of the night, I wonder what the future holds. I have an excellent legal team around me and I will fight this case with every fibre of my being and, if I lose, I will never cease fighting – secure in the knowledge that, so far as the robbery is concerned, I have right on my side.

EPILOGUE

After a four-day trial at the Kilmarnock High Court, on Thursday 16 April 1992 the jury returned from a four-hour deliberation with a verdict of 'guilty by a majority'. I was sentenced to seven years.

The jury's verdict came despite the absence of any forensic evidence linking me to the scene of the crime and in spite of the fact that a material Crown witness admitted in cross-examination that she had told lies in a crucial part of her evidence in order to save her job.

The law, both north and south of the border, states that 'a person is innocent until proven guilty beyond all reasonable doubt to a jury of his peers'. That legal theory, however, is not easily reconcilable with Scottish legal practice, where only 51 per cent of the jury need be satisfied in order to bring about a conviction. Where 49 per cent of the jury vote to acquit, the law does not consider that to be an expression of reasonable doubt. By contrast, in England 83 per cent of the jury must agree before a majority verdict is acceptable in law. I shall never know why or how many of the jury chose to convict me, but the inconclusive nature of the majority verdict and the lack of forensic evidence against me reveal again how dangerously hit and miss our criminal justice system has become.

As to the question of an appeal, my legal team, in whom I have complete faith, inform me that there is at present little hope of success. 'I'm innocent' is an earnest expression of the truth, but as grounds of challenge it would have little effect in the Court of Appeal. My only hope is that new evidence will emerge about that fateful night of 30 June 1991.

Nineteen ninety-one was a difficult year for me, but I have

learnt many lessons from it. I've always been a fighter, and no matter how difficult I may find this seven-year sentence to accept, I am already hard at work on my next book and more will follow.

As the last twelve months have demonstrated to me, in a painfully self-evident way, we never know what the future holds, but I will continue to move forward, determined always to do what I can to add to the penal debate in what I hope will be a positive, constructive and productive way.

Mark Leech
H M Prison, Barlinnie
20 April 1992